The Revelation of Music

Learning to Love the Classics

Robert Danziger

Jordan Press
New Haven 1991

Library of Congress Catalog Card Number 91-90208

ISBN 0-9613427-6-5

Published by and available from:

JORDAN PRESS
359 Central Avenue
New Haven, CT 06515

Dedicated to my father in honor of his reaching
seventy and to my mother in honor of putting
up with him while he got there.

Acknowledgments

For editing and suggestions, and for being good friends in rough times, my gratitude to my colleagues Professors Richard DeBaise, Terrence Greenawalt and Chad Hardin. For advice, encouragement, and listening to book talk, thanks to Meryl and Peter Shier, Ken Rosenthal, Kathy Forman, and my wife, Merrill.

TABLE OF CONTENTS

A Note To The Professor:

What we have here is a book that is deliberately more basic; shorter, less technical, and conspicuously lacking in musical examples. At first glance this may seem to indicate a lack of appreciation for the importance of actually listening - reading a hundred books will mean nothing without experiencing the music itself.

In fact the decision not to refer to specific pieces was made, on the contrary, in deference to the overriding importance of presenting music to the class. This is something that should be controlled by the professor rather than the text. It should depend on the opportunities current for attending live performances and it should allow the professor to vary the choice of literature so that he or she can face the new semester with a real enthusiasm that comes with the prospect of contemplating a choice of literature that is interesting, engaging, and probably not the exact same pieces done last semester and the semester before that.

Some material can be presented through assigned reading in the text; other things are much better presented in class by the professor. Naturally there is some overlap, but because this is a text intended to be used in conjunction with classroom presentation, we have not tried to do everything. Your lectures can be more than reviewing the reading because we have left room to teach. This is a text for the professor who wants to keep a good deal of control and responsibility, a text intended not to overwhelm your course.

INTRODUCTION

TO-DAY AND THEE

The appointed winners in a long-stretch'd game;
The course of time and nations-Egypt, India, Greece and Rome;
The past entire, with all its heros, histories, arts, experiments,
Its store of songs, inventions, voyages, teachers, books,
Garner'd for now and thee--To think of it!
The hierdom all converged in thee!

Walt Whitman

In any consideration of music, aesthetics and the appreciation of music, a central question must be: Which music? Every culture, as far as we know, and every time period, has had its own version of what constitutes good music.

As highly democratic thinkers, we would like to give all kinds of music equal consideration. "Who is to say", we ask, "that our music is better than that found in other times and places?" And yet who has the time to experience, in any meaningful way, even a fraction of the different kinds of music that have adorned and illuminated human existence in all its manifestations? Choices must be made.

The choices are not easy. In our age of international communications, we, in the West, have heard the alluring sounds from around the globe. And beyond just exotic sounds, we know that this music offers spiritual riches. In our willingness to be fair and open-minded, however, and despite the attraction of the exotic, we must recognize that something very unusual happened in western civilization in the course of the last several hundred years.

Consider the musicians who lived and worked within a span of one hundred years and a distance of five hundred miles from a point represented by the death of J.S. Bach in 1750, Leipzig, Germany: Handel, Vivaldi, Telemann, Haydn,   Mozart,   Schubert,   Beethoven,   Schumann, Mendelssohn, Verdi, Berlioz, Brahms.   Even the least initiated will recognize among these, the names of musical giants.   Certainly they were geniuses.   But, they were geniuses at the right time and the right place! A confluence occurred, a flowering, a synergism.   Western classical music   reached   heights   of   sublime   perfection,   and sophistication. It is difficult, if not impossible, to debate relative merits of so subjective a thing as music, but it is even more difficult to deny that something special happened here in Western music.

It is ironic that, at a time when we in the West may tend to overlook our own miraculous heritage, the enlightened in other parts of the world have found it. In Japan, western art music is pursued with passionate enthusiasm, not by just a few, but by many.   There are widespread, joyous performances of masterworks like the Beethoven *Ninth Symphony*, not only by the new Japanese professional, Western-style performing ensembles, but also by amateur community groups.

There are those who complain that our art music establishments; symphony orchestras, opera houses, concert halls, etc., are museums, so to speak, largely offering music of past ages. Well, to an extent this is true. But what glories are to be experienced in these museums of sound! And what concept, if not that of an excellent museum, offers more that is civilized and uplifting to those who are intellectually alive?

The aim of this book is a limited one: To introduce the reader to the joys and beauties of art music; not to provide a complete picture of music history, or to cover popular music, or to survey music from around the world. A look at the arts and leisure section of the Sunday New York Times will show that a great deal of art music is available and in great variety. New York, of course, is a big city, but smaller urban centers everywhere, through community concert series, local symphony orchestras, touring orchestras, etc., echo what we see offered in the Times.

Recent decades have seen the scope of this repertoire grow to include a broader spectrum and to extend farther back in time, but still, the great majority of art music readily available to us dates from the last four centuries; the periods of music we call Baroque, Classical, Romantic and Modern.

Although it is frequently argued that this is unjustly limited, there are some reasonable explanations. For one thing music created in this time was largely intended for listening to, probably by a large audience, as opposed to much music from different times and places which may have been intended for other purposes: to dance to, to worship by, or for the pleasure of the performers rather than for listeners.

It is the author's aim to provide the reader with the means and the inclination to partake of the bounty of music that is currently and readily available in our concert halls, on radio, audio and video media. Although it is admittedly a limited goal, it includes a great deal; orchestral music, choral music, opera, chamber music, etc.

There are many who claim that partaking of art music allows them to meet the challenges of life; that it lifts them, comforts them, inspires them and enriches their lives. Is this true, and, if so, why for some people and not for others? These will be central questions in the pages ahead. If the reader, with the help of this book can once scratch the surface of the greatest of our art music treasures and glimpse the deep joys and satisfactions therein, our purpose will be served. From that point it becomes, for the enlightened listener, a question of how best to divide limited time among unlimited musical possibilities.

> *"The appointed winners in a long-stretch'd game;...*
> *The past entire, with all ... Its store of songs, ...*
> *Garner'd for now and thee--To think of it!*
> *The hierdom all converged in thee!"*

CHAPTER ONE

An Approach To Listening

It would seem that listening to music should really not be difficult. Why is the subject so fraught with problems, prejudices and stumbling blocks? You hear music and you like it or you don't. Simple! Nobody can tell you what you do like or what you should like. That's the whole idea of taste. It is personal and natural. Right?... Well, in fact it is not really so simple. There are lots of things that complicate this subject; the type of music for one thing. Some music is, by nature, easier to like, more immediately attractive and therefore more popular. As a matter of fact this is where "popular music" gets its name.

In the introduction to this book, popular music was on the list of things that would not be given any significant attention. There are some good reasons for not teaching, studying and learning about popular music in the way that we sometimes need to with art music. Popular music is popular. By its very nature it is known by many and known quite well. If this were not true it would not be popular music. It is widely available: A great many radio stations, MTV, retail stores and concerts are devoted to this music. You don't need to be taught where to find popular music. It is everywhere. Many radio stations are dedicated to keeping up with not just what is generally popular, but exactly the order of how popular each song is on a daily basis: the top forty system.

When a tune gets to be number one people love to hear it and it has a powerful effect on them. They listen and drain the tune of everything that it has to offer. (This, incidentally, explains the relatively short life span of popular music.) This is music that does not demand intense contemplation, analysis or study. We are not required to dig through multiple layers of meaning. This is a good thing about popular music: What it has - it gives. It communicates easily, it does not hold back; compared to art music, it is very, very efficient.

There are, on the other hand, those who claim to have found something deeper; music that offers profound satisfaction - beyond what is offered by popular music. They report transcendental experiences with great music; they claim that it uplifts them and enriches their lives. Is this true, or is it some sort of social hoax: nobody really likes art music, they just claim to in order to make themselves appear cultured, classy and possessed of superior sensitivity? Or maybe it is true that some find these things in great music and some do not. It's in the genes somehow and you either like it or you don't. Musicians like art music. They understand it, therefore they enjoy it. Could it be that musical talent or training is the key?

The author believes that there are answers to some of these questions:

- Although there are many who claim to enjoy art music and really do not, there are also many, millions in fact, who honestly find tremendous joy in art music.

- Although it may not be true that art music is for everybody, it *is* for a great many people that have difficulty finding it on their own. If you are interested enough to give art music a chance, you almost certainly have the capacity to appreciate and enjoy it. Genes, taste, natural tendencies and abilities have a lot less to do with this than is commonly believed.

- You don't need to be a trained or literate musician to enjoy art music. Great music is very deeply felt by many who cannot sing, play, or read a note.

Pop Vs. Art Music

One great advantage that popular music has is not so much in the content of the music as it is in the format. Pop and rock tunes are usually between two and four minutes in length. The average work of art music is considerably longer, some extending over hours. Because of its compact format, popular music can be repeated frequently. This is, after all, how a song achieves popularity: It is heard, then heard again; we start to recognize it;

it grows on us; we hear it a few times more and we really start to like it, etc. This process is much more difficult with art music. It would involve a huge commitment of time to become as familiar with a symphony as we are with a pop or rock tune at the height of its popularity.

It happens frequently that an individual feels an interest in art music and determines to give it a try. Most often the experiment results in a few minutes of enjoying the refined sounds, followed by long stretches of heavy boredom. The assumption follows that either something is wrong with the music or something is wrong with the listener - in either case, it is not working and not worth it - experiment over.

Repeated Listening

The first and by far the most important technique for opening the door to great music is repetition. The listener must resist what seems an obvious conclusion; that when you have heard a piece once, you know it. Reserve judgement until you have heard the piece several times. This is not easy to do, and, in the beginning, requires a kind of trust. Take comfort in the idea that the rewards will be well worth the time and effort.

Plan to listen to each section several times; five or six is a number that usually works. You need not sit absolutely still for each of these listenings. Treat them as familiariza-tion sessions. You will find that an amazing process starts to work. You will begin to hear wonderful melodies and harmonies in what at first appeared to be barren stretches.

The work will appear to grow in beauty, meaning, clarity and expressive power. You will wonder how you could have missed these things the first time through.

This commitment to repeated listening is the single most important concept you will learn to reveal the riches of art music. It is as close a thing to magic as you will find. If you learn nothing else, this technique alone can serve to unlock the world of great music.

Sound Quality

Reproducing art music accurately can be challenging; more so than pop or rock which grew out of, and is designed for, electronic media. Much of art music, both vocal and instrumental, was created for live performance without amplification; it involves extreme contrasts of loud and soft and frequently involves extreme ranges of high and low. Shortcomings in either the recording or the playback medium can result in various kinds of distortion and can make listening highly unpleasant. Many who object to the sound of art music have never experienced it in a valid, distortion free forum. With the advent today of digital sound this should become less of a problem than it has been. Still, care needs to be taken to insure good sound. Chapter Eleven will address this issue in detail.

Meaning In Music

This is music from different times and places. It has universal things to say to us, but these things often need some degree of initial translation. Invariably, great composers were great thinkers, and they rarely wrote music just for the sound of it without having something in mind to express. In opera it is the story, and all the emotions inherent therein; in the art song it is the poetry. Even in seemingly abstract works such as symphonies and sonatas, we usually find that something is being expressed.

Ultimately the work must communicate on its own. Either it will succeed at conveying the feelings in the composers mind or it will fail but it almost always makes the process of coming to understand and appreciate a work, faster, easier, and more powerful if the listener can determine what it was that the composer intended. It is not as important, but another good reason for looking into this is simply that it is interesting. Especially when we come to love a work of music, we have a very natural and healthy urge to learn about the piece. An extension of this is to learn about the life and character of the composer. If you are so inclined, the many excellent biographies available are fascinating reading and often shed interesting light on the feelings and ideas that a composer strove to express through sound.

The great composers usually worked very hard at expressing ideas through music. We have evidence, in their own words, that they expected the most intelligent and discerning among listeners to find these connections. Example: The *Egmont Overture* by Beethoven, based on the true story of the heroic Count Egmont. The Count chose to be put to death at the hands of his country's invaders rather than betray his people. To be sure, the music clearly conveys the general feeling of heroism, brutality, tragedy and good and evil. But the diligent listener who has taken the trouble to know the story in detail and who is listening carefully, will also find revealed the exact moment when Beethoven explicitly depicts the blow of the executioner's axe as Egmont is decapitated; a chilling and powerful effect - if the listener is prepared to find it.

If the piece is *about* something, usually indicated in the title (we say that this is **program music**), find out what it is and as much as you can about it. This involves effort, but the rewards are well worth it. Details on exactly how to go about finding these things will be presented throughout this book. In general, however, the first place to look is on material that comes with recordings, liner notes, or, in the case of a live performance, in the notes usually included in the program. On some listenings you will probably just want to listen without having to read or think. That's fine - but make it a point, for at least some of the sessions, to carefully and energetically follow whatever description or information you have found.

The natural tendency is to read through the material before listening, get a general idea what it says, and then close your eyes and listen. In most cases this does not really work. We don't remember enough to make connections, our minds wander and we spend a good deal of the time in daydreaming; a pleasant prospect sometimes, but not what we are after here. The best advice is simple: read over the material and then listen hard, following the description slowly, item by item, focusing attention to hear exactly when the events or effects described occur.

If, in the case of vocal music, the piece has words, find out what they are - read them - even study them. Under no circumstances should a diligent listener depend on the performance to convey words. This is obviously true if the text is in a foreign language, but also true if the language is your own. Singing does not work to communicate words: If you don't know what the words are, you will not get them by listening to the singers.

Some of this advice may seem obvious. In practice however it is most often sadly ignored. Diligence in this area can make a tremendous difference in the ability to really connect with a piece. Underlying all of these points is the idea that, if the listener's mind is focused and engaged, it will be much easier for the purely musical aspects to have an effect.

What, then, if we can not determine that the piece is about anything? (We call this **absolute music**, the opposite of program music). The idea in this case is to focus attention on what is happening in purely musical terms. This is new territory for most listeners and needs some explanation.

Making A Blueprint For Music

Most recordings will indicate the length of the works and sections. If you can not find this, use one of the first listenings to get an accurate timing in minutes and seconds. Divide a sheet of paper into sections representing minutes. A piece lasting six minutes might be set up like this:

0:00	3:00
0:30	3:30
1:00	4:00
1:30	4:30
2:00	5:00
2:30	5:30
3:00	6:00

Notice that we start from zero, not from one.

While listening to the piece, keep track of the time and write down anything you can - anything that describes what you are hearing. Is the music loud, soft, getting softer? Is it angry, sad or a combination? Describe the texture: Is it busy? One melody or more? Is it jagged or smooth?

If you do not know how to accurately describe what you are hearing, write down anything that comes to mind. Maybe it sounds green or purple. If words fail, try drawing lines, circles, squiggles, whatever. The idea here is not to come up with correct answers, but to come up with *something*; because one of the most important things we need to determine is if and when that something comes back. And if it does, is it exactly the same or somehow different? These are the central questions. Are there repetitions, similarities, contrasts? Does the character or musical material change? Where and how?

Other important questions to consider: Does the piece divide into several main sections? How many are there, two, three, four? How many melodies are there? Which are main and which are secondary? Labeling the important melodies - or we can use the term **themes** (A,B,C, etc.) - is the best and quickest way to get your outline to take shape. How about accompaniments? Are any of the identifiable elements combined or juxtaposed in different ways?

The experienced and educated listener (this will be you at the end of this semester) will get a quicker start on developing an outline because the title of a work will usually provide indications of the form. If you are listening, for example, to a work that is marked "*rondo,*" you will expect a main theme to recur frequently. The chapters on vocal and instrumental forms in this book will provide a basis for knowing what to expect in a given work.

There can be something highly satisfying about working on an outline of this type. It is a blend of discovery and creativity, a posthumous cross-cultural collaboration with the composer. What you arrive at will be your personal interpretation, as detailed and artistic as you care to make it.

On the other hand, creating a worthy outline is a challenging job and not always accomplished without frustrations. The first time through usually yields a motley collection of words and symbols with little or no organization. Repeating the process with patience and persistence, however, will usually allow the structure of the work to reveal itself.

Although there is a great deal ahead in this book, by far the most important ideas are those you have just read. You will not know this, however, unless you take action and try these techniques for yourself. When, through the conscious application of these principles, you have once broken the shell of a great masterpiece of music, only then will the full impact of the value, the significance, and the potential for an esthetically enriched life become a reality.

CHAPTER TWO

Materials Of Music

Part One - The System of Pitches

Music depends upon sound, and all sound is a result of vibration. In the twentieth century some composers considered any sound, or even the absence of sound, to be legitimate material for composing music. In these works, still usually considered radical, little or no distinction is made between musical sound and noise. Much more commonly, music uses a particular kind of sound. When a bucket of nails falls down a flight of stairs, the resulting *noise* is highly complex, inconsistent and unpredictable. In contrast, a note played on a flute has characteristics that we usually associate with music. We can think of these as the characteristics of musical sound. Essentially, there are four: pitch, duration, loudness and tone color.

The Characteristics Of Musical Sound

PITCH

Pitch is the characteristic of sound that we recognize as highness or lowness: Men's voices are usually lower pitched than women's; birds tweet at high pitch while the extreme left-hand notes of the piano keyboard give us low pitches.

All sound is vibration, and pitch is a function of the frequency of vibration - high frequency yields high pitch, low frequency, low pitch.   Pitch is measured in vibrations per second.

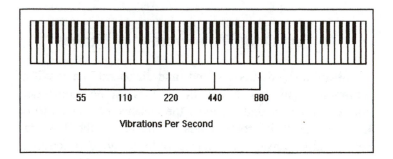

Since no assumption is made that the reader has music reading skills, the use of music notation will be avoided. Whenever possible graphic depiction of pitches and ranges will be presented in terms of the piano keyboard.   It is recommended that the reader find a piano and experiment to establish a concept of the relative highness and lowness at different levels on the keyboard.

DURATION

Duration is simply how long the sound lasts; it can be very short, very long, or anything in between.

LOUDNESS

The loudness or softness of a sound is the third characteristic. Musicians refer to the scope of loud and soft as "**dynamics**."

TONE COLOR

Tone color is also known by the French term "*timbre.*" Even if all other characteristics of sound are identical, that is, if two notes are of the same duration, the same pitch, and the same loudness, but are played on different instruments, a trumpet and a guitar for instance, we can still differentiate between the two because each has its own particular tone color.

The Pendulum And The Vibrating String

Experimenting with a pendulum, simply made from a weight and a length of string, can be helpful in considering the characteristics of sound. Allowing a weight to hang from about one foot of string, start the pendulum swinging. You will observe that, regardless of how small or large the arc, the frequency of the swings or cycles per minute remains the same. Swinging the weight with more force will make the arc of the swing, or the *amplitude,* greater, but will not effect the frequency.

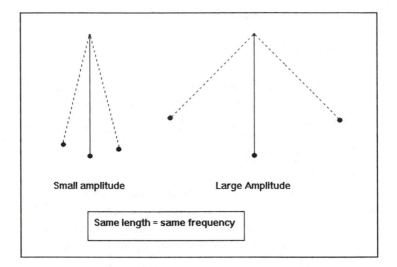

The way to change the frequency, of course, is to change the length of the string

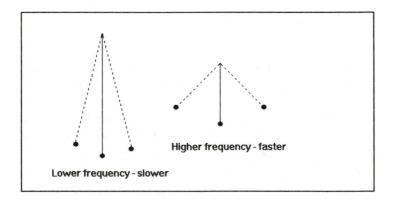

The shorter the string, the higher the frequency, the longer the string the lower the frequency.

If we now consider an arrangement found in any number of stringed instruments - a string stretched between two fixed points - we will find that the vibrations are at a higher rate, falling in the range of frequencies audible to humans as sound. Principles similar to those governing the pendulum still apply:

1.   A given length of string will vibrate at a fixed frequency - although considerably faster than the pendulum, and therefore better expressed in cycles per second rather than cycles per minute. We perceive this as pitch, or the element of highness and lowness in musical sound.

2.   Shortening the length of a string will cause it to vibrate faster, producing a higher pitch. Lengthening will cause a slower frequency and a lower pitch. (Tightening and loosening of tension on the string will also serve to change pitch, but this technique is difficult to control and used less frequently in the actual making of music.)

3.   Plucking the string harder or more gently will not change the frequency, but will affect the amplitude of the vibration, causing the sound to be respectively louder or softer.

So far, nothing has been said about the relationship of the fourth characteristic of sound, tone color, to the vibrating string. For this, we need to consider the phenomenon called **overtones.**

Overtones

At the same time that a string is vibrating as a whole, it is also vibrating in parts; halves, thirds, etc.

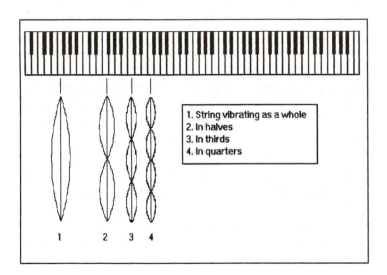

1. String vibrating as a whole
2. In halves
3. In thirds
4. In quarters

Although the pattern of these overtones is fixed by natural law, the relative strength or prominence of the individual partials varies with different instruments. The overtones of a piano string, for instance, would differ from those of a guitar. It is this phenomenon that governs tone color, allowing us to distinguish between instruments and voices.

In wind instruments, a column of air rather than a string serves as the vibrating medium, subject to the same laws of physics that govern the vibrating string.

The Phenomenon of the Octave

A closer look at the overtone series brings to light a concept of great significance in the music system. A string vibrating as a whole gives the **fundamental** frequency. For example, a string vibrating at the fundamental frequency of 110 cycles per second produces a sound we would call "low"; it lies low in the range of the average male voice. The next possible subdivision, or partial, results from the string vibrating in halves, producing a pitch recognizably higher, lying low in the range of the average female voice.

This first partial vibrates at the rate of 220 cycles per second, exactly twice the rate of the fundamental. The two resulting notes, 110 c.p.s. and 220 c.p.s., vibrating at a ratio of one to two, produces the phenomenon known as an **octave**.

These two notes, though one is noticeably higher than the other, share a "family resemblance"; they sound strongly related; they sound like higher and lower versions of the same note, and they have a restful, comfortable sound, called **consonance**. Changing either of the pitches to a note slightly higher or lower completely destroys this octave relationship and causes **dissonance** rather than consonance, a jarring, unsettled sound.

Division of the Octave

Since octaves can be found either higher or lower for any given pitch by doubling or halving the frequency of vibration, it can be seen that they occur regularly throughout the range of audible sounds.

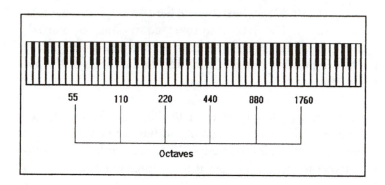

The Dominant

Having established that the first two tones of the overtone series are the fundamental and its higher octave, let us consider the next note in the series. This is produced by the string (or the air column, in a wind instrument) vibrating in thirds.

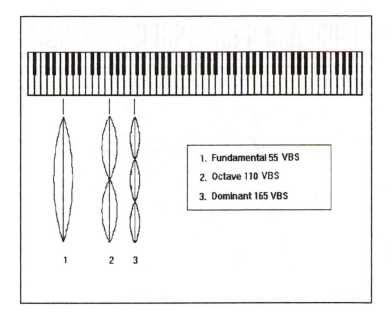

1. Fundamental 55 VBS
2. Octave 110 VBS
3. Dominant 165 VBS

The resulting tone, called the **dominant**, is another phenomenon of great significance in the music system. Whereas octaves are perceived as higher and lower versions of the same note, the dominant provides a new note. These two notes establish what is known as a tonic-dominant relationship, the fundamental being the **tonic**. The relationship of the tonic and dominant notes are in a two to three ratio.

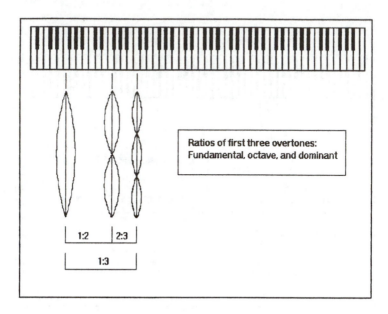

Ratios of first three overtones:
Fundamental, octave, and dominant

1:2   2:3

1:3

When these notes are heard one after the other, the tonic gives the impression of being stable and resolved, a feeling of "homeness;" the dominant gives a feeling of being unstable, away from home, and requiring resolution to the tonic.   This pulling force, back to the tonic, can be thought of as a sort of musical gravity. · It is called **tonality**.

Although the range of audible frequencies is capable of being divided into an infinite number of individual pitches. A look at any standard keyboard reveals that, in practice, each octave is divided into twelve individual notes. Since these notes are the actual "building blocks" of music, the question of how this division of the octave came about is an important one. It might be assumed that this division of the musical "spectrum" into our system of exactly twelve individual notes has been accomplished somewhat arbitrarily, that we have become accustomed or conditioned over the years to accept this particular division, but that others might have developed just as naturally. Why not have the octave divided into 13 notes, or 17, or maybe fewer, 7, or 979? The same object that we call "apple" in English is called "*pomme*" in French; The sound, "*he*" in Hebrew translates as "she" in English. Is it not likely, then, that we would find the same kinds of cultural or geographical differences in how the octave is divided? In fact, what we do find is a natural "system" that dictates our 12 notes; a system wonderfully elegant in construction and one that is essentially universal.

Generating the Chromatic Scale

We have established two notes: the tonic and a new note, the dominant. Suppose that we treat the dominant as a fundamental. From that, a new dominant can be generated, establishing a third note. Repeating the process provides a fourth note, then a fifth, and so on. Twelve different notes can be generated in this way. The thirteenth note, however, is a duplication, in a higher octave, of the original fundamental. Continuing the process only duplicates the entire series. And so, by establishing a cycle of tonics and dominants and then arranging the twelve resulting notes in a one octave range, our entire musical system can be generated. This series of all twelve notes arranged by pitch in ascending or descending order is called a **chromatic scale**.

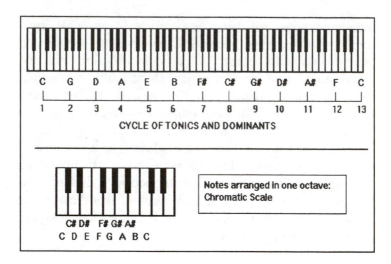

The chromatic scale provides a complete system, essentially all the notes needed for conventional music making. It is possible to produce tones that are subdivisions or in-between the notes of the chromatic scale. We find this particularly in jazz and music of the Eastern part of the world, but this is usually perceived by the listener as stretching or bending of the chromatic scale, rather than actual additional notes.

- SCALE: A series of pitches that proceeds up or down according to a prescribed pattern.   A pitch vocabulary for music.

The chromatic scale includes all 12 notes of our musical system.   By itself, however, this scale of evenly and equally spaced notes does not serve well as the functional basis for an actual musical work.   For this, one of a number of different scales, consisting of fewer notes, is required.

Over the centuries, and in different parts of the world, many different kinds of scales have been and continue to be used, but since the era in music history known as **High Baroque** (about 1700), the vast majority of music has been based on the **major scale** and its relative, the **minor scale**.

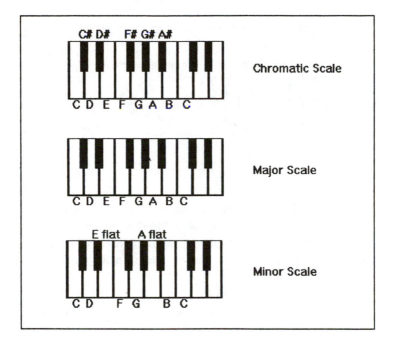

The "major" is the most frequently used of scales, commonly recognizable, even to non musicians, as "the scale." In the system developed in Italy for reading music, known as *Solfeggio*, the major scale would be sung using the syllables *do re mi fa sol la ti do.*

Further consideration of the major scale can show several interesting things:

1.   We can see that the particular appearance of the modern musical keyboard is tied to the prevalence of the major scale. It is the chromatic scale, with the notes of the major scale forward in white, and the remaining notes, those not included in the major scale, pushed back and represented in black.

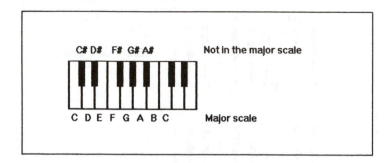

2.   The major scale, for the most part, follows the chromatic scale in a play-one-skip-one pattern.   This interval, every other chromatic note, is termed a "whole step." The notes then of the chromatic scale are termed "half steps."

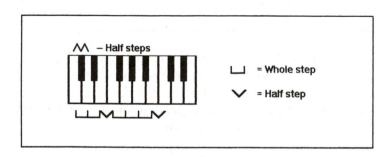

3. In musical terminology notes are referred to by their position in the major rather than the chromatic scale. The major scale consists of seven notes, the eighth being an octave of the first. We think of the octave as the eighth note of the major scale rather than the thirteenth note of the chromatic scale. Thus the name "octave" from the Latin root *Octus* or Eight.

Construction Of The Major And Minor Scales

Scales and modes are built upon patterns of whole steps and half steps.

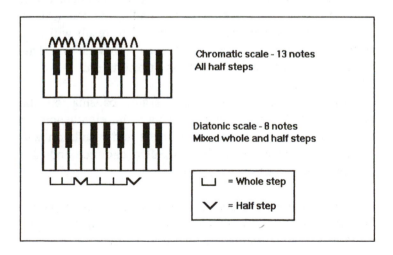

Chromatic scale - 13 notes
All half steps

Diatonic scale - 8 notes
Mixed whole and half steps

⎵ = Whole step

∨ = Half step

• DIATONIC: Made up of only the notes of the prevailing key or scale. The opposite of "chromatic."

Major and minor are examples of "diatonic scales." Diatonic scales are extracted from the chromatic scale.

Tonality And Scales (Melodic Tonality)

A sense of musical gravity or homeness, called **tonality**, can result from just two notes, the tonic and dominant. One of the reasons that music is generally not built on the chromatic scale is that this scale, with its equal and evenly spaced notes, does not establish any home base or feeling of tonality. The major and minor scales, on the other hand, create a very strong feeling of tonality. To experience this you need only play or sing the major scale, either ascending or descending, but ending on the seventh note, that is, one note before the end. The result will be a strong feeling of incompleteness or lack of resolution. This series of notes demands completion or resolution.

Now sing or play the same scale, pausing on the seventh note, but then concluding with the eighth note or tonic. A feeling of arrival, fulfillment and resolution will result. This feeling of arrival is called **cadence** and also occurs at the end of musical phrases.

The term **key** is practically synonymous with tonality. We speak of a work being in the "key" of C major, meaning it is built on the C major scale or tonality.

Part Two - Texture

Monophony

The simplest musical texture is **monophony**, literally "one voice" music. An example would be one person singing alone or playing a "one note at a time" instrument such as the flute (not guitar or piano, as these instruments usually play several notes at a time). No accompaniment is involved and nothing we would call "harmony." Monophonic music might, in some instances include more than one performer, however. **Gregorian Chant**, music of the early Christian Church, for instance, is usually heard sung by a group of Monks. But they sing in unison, the same note at the same time; there is only one line of music.

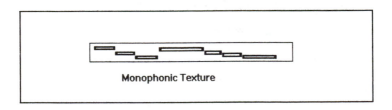

Monophonic Texture

Polyphony

Polyphony is music that is perceived to consist of more than one melody. A "round", such as "Row, Row, Row, Your Boat", wherein the tune is begun at different times by different singers or groups of singers, can call this to mind. In the case of a round, it is the same melody that occurs at different times. In most polyphony, the melodies are not the same, although, of course, they would be constructed so as to fit together in a way that is musically satisfying. "Countermelodies" and "descants" are two specific kinds of polyphony, but, more often, polyphony involves two, three, or more simultaneously heard lines of music, relatively equal in importance.

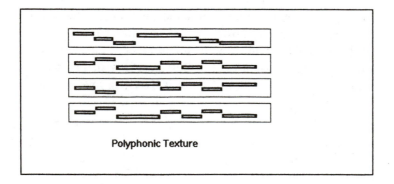

Polyphonic Texture

Homophony

Although homophony is the most common type of music we hear, it is, at the same time, the most difficult to describe. It is music that is perceived as a melody with accompaniment. An example would be someone singing and strumming chords on a guitar for accompaniment.

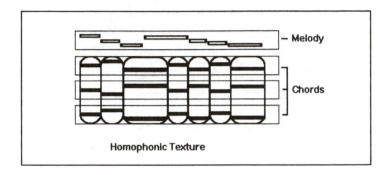

Homophonic Texture

It is not always easy to distinguish homophony from polyphony because the determining factor is how it is perceived by the individual. The same arrangement of pitches might be perceived as one or the other by different listeners.

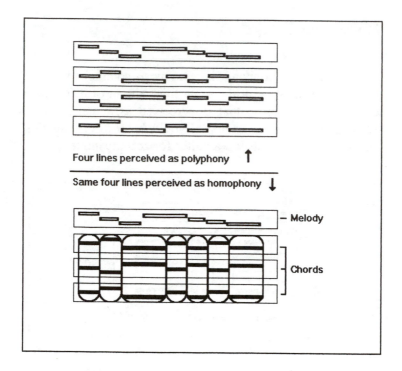

Four lines perceived as polyphony ↑

Same four lines perceived as homophony ↓

— Melody

Chords

It is important to understand that, although it is possible to find music that is completely homophonic, or completely polyphonic, more often the textures are blended, alternated or combined, and we find it to be a matter of degree. We might perceive a piece to be largely homophonic, but with some elements of polyphony or vice versa. Or, the texture might shift as the work progresses, from more homophonic to more polyphonic, for example.

Chords

When we perceive a musical section as sounding homophonic as opposed to polyphonic it is because we hear certain combinations of notes as blocks or units. We refer to these as **"chords"** and they are built on a play-one, skip-one pattern of the notes of the diatonic scale (not the chromatic scale).

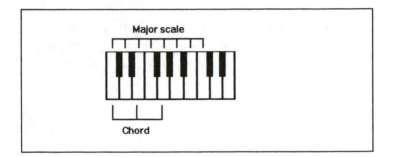

Music majors take a course in "Harmony," where they learn to work with chords, the different forms and qualities possible, and how they proceed from one chord to the other in the course of a composition. Basic chords consist of three notes, called a **triad**, with additional notes added in more advanced harmonic idioms. A chord can be built on any note of the scale.

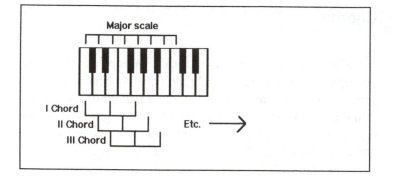

Although harmonization can be a highly complex art, a great deal can be done with three basic chords. These are the tonic or I chord, the dominant or V chord, and the sub-dominant or IV chord.

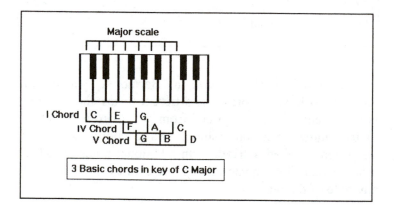

3 Basic chords in key of C Major

Unless they happen to be complex or unusual, folk and popular melodies and most rock music can be provided with a basic harmonization using only these three basic chords. Fitting these chords to melodies is a key part of being able to play by ear. (It is possible for some people to develop this "feel" for chords and harmony by patient "fooling around" or experimentation with piano or guitar).

Harmonic Tonality

We have seen that there is a sense of tonality inherent in the scale and in melodies based on the scale. Tonality exists in harmony as well. A series of chords, known as a **chord progression**, should have a feeling of syntax. Certain chords followed by others sound right, others sound wrong. A satisfying chord progression carries the listener through degrees of tension and resolution culminating in a cadence. This is the harmonic counterpart to the sense of "gravity" or tonality that we find in melody.

Transposition and Modulation

By adjusting the patterns of whole steps and half steps, any scale can be constructed beginning on any note. Likewise, any melody or harmonic progression can be started on any note. (For simplicity, the illustrations in this chapter are all given in the key of C) This changing of the overall pitch level of an entire musical work is called **transposition**. We encounter this frequently in vocal music where, in order to better fit an individual voice, a singer might prefer to perform a song or aria either higher or lower than originally composed. It can also occur in instrumental music; a piece originally written for orchestra might be rewritten, or **transcribed** for band. In this case the piece may be transposed up or down to a key that better suits the range and character of the band instruments.

Like transposition, **modulation** is also a change of key, the difference being that modulation happens during the course of a composition.   The composer manipulates musical material so that the tonality or key of the piece, the center of gravity, so to speak, shifts subtly, or modulates, from the original key. This may happen a number of times in the course of longer, more complex compositions. Although modulation usually happens so smoothly as to be imperceptible to most listeners, musicians believe that this shifting away from and back to the home key establishes a largely subconscious, but important, large scale structural architecture, with increased effects of tension and resolution.

Part Three - Music In Time

Simply reading will not be enough for this section. You need to read, read out loud, recite, sing and clap. Save this section for a time when you are alone or among those who will not fear for your sanity when you do this.

Probably the most elemental characteristic of music is that it exists in time.   This can make understanding difficult; we would like to stop or freeze the music in order to contemplate it, as we do in examining a painting. But when music stops, we lose it; it is no longer music.

Rhythm (as a general term)

The word "rhythm" comes from the Greek word for "flow" and we use it to describe the flow of music through time. In general, this has to do with the length of tones, their relation to one another, and to silence. More specifically there are a few rhythmic concepts that we should be able to talk about: beat, tempo and meter.

Beat

Sing or recite the following:

Mary had a little lamb,
Little lamb, little lamb.
Mary had a little lamb,
Whose fleece was white as snow.

Try it again, this time clapping along with the ongoing, underlying pulse. Try this now.

You probably clapped in these places:

Ma ry   had   a   lit tle lamb,
>   >   >   >

Lit tle   lamb,   lit tle lamb.
>   >   >   >

```
Ma   ry   had   a   lit tle  lamb whose
>         >         >      >
```

```
fleece was white  as   snow    -
>           >          >
```

This ongoing, underlying pulse, found in almost all music, is called the **beat**.

Rhythm (another meaning)

In addition to referring to the overall concept of the flow of music in time, the term "rhythm" can also have a more specific meaning, as in the question, "What is the rhythm of this piece?

Sing or recite "Mary had..." again. This time clap on *every* syllable.

```
Ma  ry  had  a   lit tle  lamb
>   >   >    >   >   >    >
```

```
Lit tle   lamb, lit  tle   lamb
>   >     >     >    >    >
```

```
Ma  ry  had  a   lit tle  lamb whose
>   >   >    >   >   >    >    >
```

```
fleece was   white as   snow    -
>      >     >    >    >
```

This time you clapped the **rhythm** of the song.

Meter

Returning to the concept of beat, did you notice that some beats tend to be stronger, heavier or more emphasized than others? We call this **accent**. Clap the beat again. You probably found a pattern with every other beat stressed or accented:

Ma ry had a   lit tle   lamb
ONE   two   ONE   two

Lit tle lamb,   lit tle lamb
ONE   two   ONE   two

Ma ry had a   lit tle   lamb whose
ONE   two   ONE   two

fleece was white as   snow   -
ONE   two   ONE   two

This grouping of beats into regularly recurring patterns is called **meter**. Sing and clap the beat:

Did you e-ver see a lassie go
   This way and that way?
Did you e-ver see a lassie go
   This way and that?

You probably discovered a pattern like this:

```
Did you e---ver see a lassie go
3       1 2   3   1 2 3
>       >         >
```

```
        This way and that way?
        1   2   3   1   2
        >           >
```

```
Did you e---ver see a lassie go
3       1 2   3   1 2 3
>       >         >
```

```
        This way and that?
        1   2   3   1   2 3
        >           >
```

In most music we can find an underlying pattern that feels like either: ONE two, ONE two - we call this **duple meter** - or ONE two three, ONE two three, called **triple meter**. To tell one from the other, first find the strong or accented beats; then count the beats that fall between to determine if there are two for duple meter or three for triple meter. Duple meter is more common. The waltz and minuet are dance forms that use triple meter. A somewhat more complex pattern occurs when a piece is basically in duple meter but can be subdivided into groups of threes. We call this **compound meter**. *Row, Row, Row Your Boat* is an example.

```
Row     row     row  your boat
>  . .  >  . .  >  . .   >  . .
1 2 3  4 5 6  1 2 3   4 5 6
```

```
Gent--ly down  the stream
>  . .  >  . .    >  . .    >  . .
1  2 3  4  5 6   1  2 3   4  5 6
```

```
Mer-ri-ly  mer-ri-ly  mer-ri-ly mer-ri-ly
>   . .  >   . .  >   . .  >   . .
1   2 3  4   5 6 1   2 3 4   5 6
```

```
life  is but  a dream.
>  . .  >  . .  >  . .  >  . .
1  2  3  4  5  6  1  2  3  4  5  6
```

Musicians analyze, recognize, and read and write these patterns in musical notation. For listeners, even expert, enlightened listeners, this is not required. It is not necessary to know that a piece is in 6/8 meter to enjoy it. But a basic understanding of how music is organized in time is interesting in itself, makes it easier to understand what is happening in a piece, and provides the means to communicate and exchange thoughts about what we are hearing, and ultimately what we are feeling, as we listen.

CHAPTER THREE

Instruments

The number and variety of musical instruments extends broadly over history and culture. These instruments can be fascinating to consider. As a rule, the craftsmanship of the maker and the demands of shaping a vessel to produce beautiful sound combine in mysterious ways to create instruments that please the eye as well as the ear. If an instrument is very old, artistically created, or even better, both, it may be of great value to collectors as well as to musicians. Determination of an instrument's value involves more than strictly musical matters; there are considerations more in the fields of art and antiques. It is not unusual for the price of a fine instrument to climb above the hundred-thousand dollar mark. A look at one of the beautiful books on historic instruments or a catalogue from a dealer in rare instruments can show that these unique creations have an attraction that transcends the sounds they produce.

There is a widespread and unfortunate belief that learning to play an instrument is essentially for children. This is not necessarily so. Age should never prevent someone from taking up an instrument if they have the inclination. Someone who begins playing as an adult can achieve a highly satisfying level of performance.

Unsuccessful childhood experience with lessons can leave a tendency to underestimate musical ability. Adult students, with maturity, motivation, and self discipline, can often make very rapid progress. If in the course of reading the following sections, the idea of playing one of these instruments presents itself, you should know that there is every good reason to act on it.

Orchestral Strings

The orchestral strings, violin, viola, 'cello and string bass, are essentially larger and smaller versions of the same basic instrument. The violin and the 'cello, for instance, share very similar proportions, the 'cello being roughly double in size and correspondingly lower in pitch. Some small deviations from this concept will be noted in the discussion of the viola and string bass.

Although there are sections of first violins and second violins in the orchestra, the instruments in both sections are identical.

Violin
The mystery of what makes one violin sound and play better than another has intrigued musicians and consumed the energy and imagination of scientists and **luthiers** (as violin makers are

such craftsmen as Amati, Stradivari, and Guarnieri, in the northern Italian town of Cremona, are the most highly prized. Thickness of wood, proportions of the instrument, age and type of wood, and the varnish used to finish the instrument have all been experimented with extensively in efforts to solve the mystery.

Violin

From time to time it happens that a modern luthier will produce a series of particularly good sounding instruments - violinists get excited and we hear claims that the secret of the "Old Masters" has been rediscovered. Certainly some modern makers are better than others, but to date, no modern instrument has captured the excellence, the responsiveness, the depth and richness of tone of the old violins. Albert Einstein, who was an amateur violinist, and who also knew something about science, insisted that we are nowhere near commanding the sophistication required to solve the mysteries of violin making.

It is a fact that the best way to keep a fine stringed instrument healthy is to play it. The instrument is nourished by the vibration. Because of this, and very fortunately, these legendary ancient violins are on display not only to see, as in a museum, but also to hear, since they are routinely played by today's finest musicians in our major concert halls.

Usually, the same craftsmen that produced exceptional violins also built other instruments of the string family. The Library of Congress in Washington D.C. has an extraordinary set of instruments made by Antonio Stradivari; two violins, a viola and a 'cello. This makes up the instrumentation of a chamber music ensemble known as the string quartet. The finest string quartets in the world are honored with invitations to present concerts at the "Library", using these exquisite instruments.

Viola and Violin

Viola

The viola can be thought of as a larger version of the violin. An interesting situation provides the viola with its peculiar tone: Like the violin, the viola is held under the player's chin. It is, however, tuned five tones lower. If the viola were to be constructed with the same proportions as the violin, relative to the pitch of its strings, it would be somewhat too large for even the largest players. To accommodate this, the viola is built smaller, in relation to its pitch, than correct violin proportions would dictate. The result is a characteristic sound, muffled and nasal at the same time, compared to the other strings, and uniquely beautiful to hear.

'Cello

'Cello

The full name for this instrument is violoncello although the shorter term, "'cello" is more commonly used.   Violoncello, not violincello.   The 'cello is always played from a sitting position (even when the rest of the orchestra stands to play the national anthem).   In the Seventeenth Century, the instrument was held, supported by the players legs, but modern 'cellos are fitted with an endpin that extends from the instrument to the floor. The solo repertoire for the 'cello, while not as extensive as that for the violin, is still considerable, and of high quality.   The Spanish 'cellist Pablo Casals achieved legendary status in the first half of the twentieth century while today, 'cellists YoYo Ma and Lynn Harrel are highly acclaimed virtuosi.

String Bass

More diverse in form than the other members of the string family, "string bass" is a generic term for these large instruments.   Although the pitch of the strings has been standardized, shapes and sizes of the actual instruments vary considerably. We sometimes refer to them as full size, three quarter size, half size, etc., but the fact is that they come in many non-standard sizes, especially the great old basses.   While some have the usual shape in common with the violin, viola and 'cello, many have the sloping shoulders of the viols, an ancient family of string instruments related to, but distinct from, the violin family.

Diverse as well are the names we use for these instruments. They are variously referred to as: String bass, bass viol, double bass, contrabass, bass violin, or bass fiddle.   Although the electric bass, (actually an electric bass guitar), is used in modern pop and jazz, some sophisticated players still prefer the traditional string bass, sometimes fitted with an electronic pickup and usually plucked rather than bowed.

String Bass

Harp

The basic idea of the harp is very simple; a series of strings stretched on a frame with some sort of resonator box, played by plucking with the fingers. It is an instrument found in simple form from the earliest times, and, in this form, is still used in folk music around the world. In order to play all of the notes of our modern chromatic scale, however, a complex pedal mechanism is required.

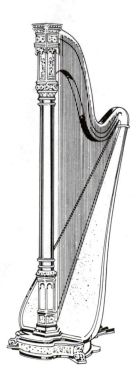

Harp

As all other members of the orchestral string section are related to the violin, the harp does not really belong in this family, but rather constitutes a separate unit in the orchestra. It was first used in the orchestra in the Romantic Period, and is considered an optional instrument called for only in large orchestrations. Usually, either one or two harps are used. The harp does not have the capacity to play loudly, and it is limited in the kinds of passages that it is well suited for. Thus a composer would not use the harp for a long-lined, singing melody, but its unique, resonant, unmistakable sound is incomparable for evoking a magical, mystical, other-worldly aura.

Orchestral Winds

Modern wind instruments are thought of as belonging to one of two categories: woodwind or brass. Originally, as the names imply, the families were distinguished by the material of which they were made. Over the years the instruments have evolved so that today all woodwinds are not made of wood. There remains, however, a real distinction between the families and it has to do with the way the instruments alter their pitch.

In wind instruments pitch depends on the length of the vibrating column of air. Most brass instruments produce different notes by opening and closing a series of valves in various combinations, which adds or subtracts lengths of tubing. The trombone, holding to an ancient technique, employs a slide mechanism to accomplish this. Woodwinds, on the other hand, effect changes in pitch as the player opens or closes a complex and extensive series of finger holes located up and down the length of the instrument.

Woodwinds

Flute

Flutes have been around in one form or other since prehistoric times. The modern form of the flute is known as the transverse flute because it is held cross-wise rather than up and down like the other woodwinds and older forms of the flute, such as the recorder. The transverse flute came into prominence in art music in the 1700s, during the late Baroque Period. The orchestra was growing larger at this time and the transverse flute had the ability to play somewhat louder than the recorder and therefore balance better in ensemble.

Piccolo and Flute

Sound on the transverse flute is produced by the very simple principle of blowing across a hole in the instrument. You have probably used this same technique to produce sound from a soda bottle. Although flutes were originally all made of wood, the orchestra has continued to grow over the years, and the trend has been away from wooden flutes, toward flutes made of metal, producing a sound with still greater carrying power. Today, in Germany and England, we still find some players who prefer the sweeter tone of wooden flutes, but they are increasingly rare.

While student-model flutes are now usually made of silver-plated brass, professional musicians use flutes made of solid silver. Some instruments are made specially for virtuoso flutists of solid gold or platinum. These metals yield a heavier, darker sound, but many players insist that silver provides the ideal, balanced flute tone.

The piccolo, found in the concert band and in large orchestras, is half the size of the flute and an octave higher, with a shrill and piercing sound in the high register. Larger members of the flute family are the alto and bass flutes. Although the voluptuous and haunting sound of these larger instruments does not carry very well, they are sometimes called for in large, modern orchestrations.

Oboe

Oboe & English Horn

Although it has a range of just over two octaves, smaller than other woodwinds, the oboe's hauntingly beautiful, penetrating sound is frequently chosen by composers to present their most expressive melodies. Double reed instruments like the oboe have existed, in simple form, since prehistoric times. In order to understand the principal of the oboe it is possible to actually make a crude but workable instrument from a drinking straw. In essence, one end of the straw is flattened out to produce a vibration when breath is applied. As in all woodwinds, pitch is governed by opening and closing a series of finger holes along the length of the tube (the body of the straw).

In the actual instrument, the reed, though it does look something like a flattened straw, is made of cane. The body of the instrument is made of ebony or grenadilla wood. The oboe has been a regular and consistent member of the orchestra since the Baroque Period. It is generally considered to be one of the more difficult instruments to play, partly due to the fact that serious oboe players must learn to make and adjust reeds, a job that is exacting, time consuming, and requiring great skill.

English Horn

The English Horn is a somewhat larger and lower version of the oboe. It differs in appearance in having a short metal tube extending to the reed and a sort of pregnant bulge at the bottom or "bell" end. The sound is less penetrating than the oboe, but more plaintive and very beautiful. It is not particularly English at all, the name being a mistranslation of "angle horn" (describing the characteristic bend in the tube leading to the reed) into the French "Cor Anglais," and then back into English again.

Clarinet
Like the oboe, the clarinet is made of ebony or granadilla wood and, like the oboe it has a generally medium-high range. Unlike the oboe, however, it employs a single reed, fixed by means of a ligature, to a mouthpiece. While the bore of the oboe is conical, that is, shaped like a long, very gradual cone, the clarinet has a cylindrical bore, producing different tonal and playing characteristics.

The result is a smoother, purer tone than the oboe, and a considerably wider range, extending both higher and lower. The well designed fingering system of the clarinet allows considerable flexibility and a wonderful liquidity of technique. Composers, therefore, frequently write rapid passages that challenge the clarinetist's agility and technical skill.

Clarinet

Of somewhat more recent origin than others in the woodwind family, the clarinet came to the orchestra in the Classical Period, around 1800, and since that time has been a regular member.

Most commonly encountered is the soprano clarinet in B flat, but there are other sizes that make up a complete family. (Although all modern wind instruments can play in all keys, the way they are constructed dictates that one scale will be most basic and natural. The different sizes in some families of instruments are distinguished by the name of this scale.) The clarinet in A is just slightly larger, and a half step lower, than the B flat. It is used frequently by orchestral players who usually carry these two sizes together in one case. The soprano clarinet in E flat, smaller, higher and shriller, is called for in large orchestrations, as is the larger E flat alto clarinet and the B flat bass clarinet. Even larger are the E flat and B flat contrabass clarinets. These behemoths, though, are likely to be found in concert bands and only rarely in orchestra.

Bass Clarinet

Bassoon And Contrabassoon

The bassoon is a double reed instrument and the bass member of the woodwind family. Because of its unique, dry, bouncing staccato, the bassoon is frequently used for funny sounding passages. But in the middle and high registers it can sing with a poignant eloquence. Like the oboe, the bassoon has a long history in the orchestra, and has been regularly called for by composers since the days of Baroque music.

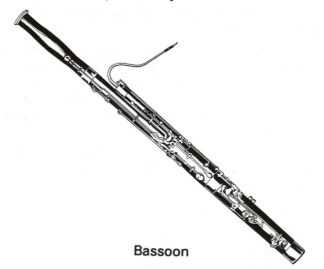

Bassoon

In order to produce the low notes in the bassoon's range, the instrument actually needs to be about nine feet in length. This would be unwieldy, and the finger holes would be too spread out to reach, even with the largest of hands. The solution was, in effect, to double the instrument back on itself, bringing the holes within reach of the fingers and making the entire arrangement more manageable. This is accomplished, in the lower section, by creating two parallel bores in one length of maple and joining them with a "U" tube. Thus the bassoon's peculiar appearance.

The contra bassoon is more than twice as long as the bassoon and plays an octave lower, producing the lowest tones in the orchestra. The contra was first used in the early 1800s, and since that time, has been called for regularly in large orchestral instrumentations.

Contra Bassoon

Brass Instruments

Trumpet
The trumpet has been around in its basic form since biblical times. In essence, it is a long cylindrical, metal tube with a cup-

like mouthpiece on one end and a flair at the other. The player makes a buzzing sound with the lips into the mouthpiece to create a vibration. The flair or bell at the other end serves to amplify the sound as it emerges.

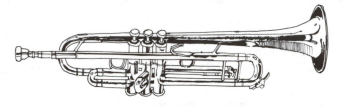

Trumpet

In simplest form, with the unbent tube extending in a straight line, the instrument is called a herald trumpet. It is associated with royal ceremonies, and still used today on occasions that demand a regal touch.

It was eventually discovered that brass instruments could be coiled into more manageable shapes without adversely affecting playing characteristics. Thus, in its modern curled oval shape, the trumpet took its place in the Baroque orchestra, even though it could only produce a limited number of notes: the notes corresponding to the overtone series.

Since the notes of the overtone series are further apart at the low end, and closer together further up, composers for the Baroque trumpet were limited to the extreme high register for melodic parts. This yielded fiendishly difficult trumpet parts, but parts that were glorious and thrilling to hear.

By about 1840 advancing technology offered an improvement for brass instruments in the form of valves. Now the player could, in effect, add and subtract lengths of tubing, making the complete chromatic scale available to the trumpet's middle and low registers. Composers could now write diatonic and even chromatic passages for the trumpet from the lowest to the highest notes. Other techniques such as trills, which on the Baroque trumpet had required a high degree of virtuosity, were now greatly facilitated.

Unfortunately, as they adjusted to the improved capabilities of valved trumpets, players in the late Nineteenth and early Twentieth Centuries lost the Baroque technique of playing in the extreme high register. This was not a major concern at the time, as Baroque music was only rarely performed in the Romantic and early Modern periods, but as interest in Baroque music rekindled, in the last fifty years, trumpeters have had to rediscover the ancient techniques for ascending into the high register.

Trumpets are made in a greater variety of sizes than any of the other orchestral instruments, and there is less agreement about when to use which size. It would not be uncommon for a professional trumpet player to own at least a half dozen instruments of different sizes and to bring an assortment of these to a rehearsal or performance. Although the trumpet in B flat is usually considered to be the standard size, orchestral players frequently prefer the slightly smaller trumpet in C. Some players prefer to switch back and forth between three or four different size instruments for different passages in a single performance, while others prefer to play the whole evening on one instrument.

The cornet and Flugelhorn are relatives of the trumpet with identical range and technical characteristics, but each with a respectively more conical (cone-like) shape, resulting in a mellower and therefore less penetrating tone. These instruments are more frequently found in the band than in the orchestra.

Because of the trumpet's powerful and sometimes awe inspiring sound, composers depend on them to carry the orchestra to glorious heights and thrilling climaxes. It is the nature of the instrument that if the trumpet player fails to negotiate a climactic high passage, or plays with less than heroic spirit, it is immediately obvious to all. This is not the instrument for an introvert or for the faint of heart.

French Horn

The French horn is like the trumpet, but longer, about 11 feet in all, and with a more exaggerated conical bore; that is, starting smaller at the mouthpiece end, and ending larger, at the bell end. The French horn is a descendant of the horn used for signalling in the hunt. The tubing was coiled into the characteristic round shape to facilitate carrying on horseback.

French Horn

A pair of French horns were the first, and frequently the only, wind instruments added to the strings in the early development of the orchestra (Baroque and Classical periods). Before the invention of valves, this "natural horn," like the trumpet, produced only the notes of the overtone series, but because of the horn's greater length, the normal playing range was higher up in the series of harmonics, allowing the composer to write complete melodies. In addition, horn players developed a technique of inserting the hand in the bell or "stopping", as it was called, to lower the pitch of naturally occurring notes in order to fill in gaps in the overtone series. The addition of valves, in the early 1800s, improved the horn's flexibility and evened out rough spots in the scale.

Although the horn is generally played in the medium to high register, the length of the tube provides a tremendous range, allowing expert players to produce extremely low notes. With the usual section of four horns in the modern orchestra, the full spectrum of horn tone is available and composers often write passages in four parts for horns alone.

The rich, dark, distant, covered sound of the French horn in slow, singing melodies can be beautifully affecting. On the other hand, the power of the horn section playing full force is overwhelming when used to convey musical expressions of elation, triumph, heroism, tragedy, or almost any of the strongest emotions.

Trombone

The trombone is twice as long as the trumpet and one octave lower. It is the only modern brass instrument to use a slide mechanism for lengthening and shortening the tube to change pitch.

The trombone has a cylindrical bore. It must have, in order for the slide mechanism to work: one section of tubing fitting precisely over another section of just slightly smaller diameter. This slide mechanism was developed long before the valves used in other modern brasses, and the slide trombone, in something very close to its modern form, has been in use since the Middle Ages.   An ancient form of the trombone was called the "sackbut."

Trombone

The trombone had been traditionally associated with funeral music, and its first use in orchestra in the Classical Period, in large works of a sombre, religious nature, reflected this. In the larger orchestra, common in the romantic and modern eras, the trombone is a more usual presence. Three trombones, usually combined with the tuba, are used by composers to complete the low end of the brass choir and to provide a sound of great weight and power to full orchestrations.

Because of its slide mechanism, the trombone can accomplish a very effective characteristic glissando or "smear," a gradual sliding up or down in pitch, through a series of notes. Composers make use of this for special and comic effects.

Tuba

The tuba, though it too comes in different sizes, is most commonly an octave lower than the trombone and two octaves lower than the trumpet. It is the bass of the brass family and is capable of a great volume of sound. Three valves, much like the trumpet's, are used to affect changes in pitch. It has been in use since the mid 1800s, but only in the largest orchestrations .

Tuba

Percussion

In general, the percussion section of the orchestra includes instruments that are played by striking, and includes a far greater number of instruments than any of the other sections. They fall into two large categories, tuned and untuned. The tuned category includes bells, xylophone-like instruments and timpani. Through the Baroque and Classical Periods, the only percussion instruments regularly found in the orchestra were the timpani, or kettle drums.   As the name implies, they look like kettles with calf-skin stretched across the opening and produce low sonorous tones that lend a solid foundation to the orchestra. They are also capable of great power.

Timpani

The untuned class of percussion instruments includes triangle, tambourine, snare drum, gong, and literally hundreds of other instruments.   Included are sound-effect like devices such as bird whistles, wind machines, whips, etc.

The piano is often found as a solo instrument, accompanied by orchestra, in a performance of one of the many concertos written for it.   But as an orchestral instrument, in Twentieth Century orchestrations, the piano, like other keyboard instruments, is considered a member of the percussion section.

Keyboard Instruments

Harpsichord
Before the invention of the piano, that is, through the Baroque Period, the harpsichord and the organ were the main keyboard instruments. Because of the organs great size, the harpsichord was a practical choice for most demands and was widely used. Sound was produced on the harpsichord by a mechanism that plucked the strings with a quill or leather plectrum. This system had a disadvantage in that the player could not vary dynamics; all notes were equally loud, but this was compensated for in larger harpsichords by a mechanism for adding and subtracting ranks of strings.

Harpsichord

The development of the piano, in which the strings were struck by hammers rather than plucked, did allow for a range of dynamics; thus the original full name of the instrument: Pianoforte or "soft-loud," ("piano" is an abbreviation of this).

With its ability to play many notes at once in a full range of dynamics, it is the most complete of instruments, able, by itself, to hold the interest of composers, performers and listeners. Thus the piano has an unparalleled repertoire of solo works, sonatas and concertos.

The organ, being a larger instrument, shares some of the piano's scope in terms of being complete and self-sufficient, but because the organ requires a very large space, the piano emerged as a much more practical choice for individuals and families, as it fits in almost any living area.

Grand Piano

The modern piano comes in many sizes from small, spinet models to immense concert grands. The grand piano configuration, though it requires more space, has a superior action (the way the keys feel and respond) and is always used by concert pianists due to the more direct horizontal linkage from the key to the hammer which strikes the string.

Organ

From the Baroque period until mid-twentieth century, the term **organ** referred to a large instrument in which the sound was produced by pumping air through sets of tuned and voiced pipes. With the advent of electricity, a species of electronic organ appeared. Because of this new instrument's smaller size and smaller cost, it became popular in small churches and homes. It is this electronic instrument which many of us think of as the organ. This is somewhat unfortunate in that while the newer instrument does resemble the sound of the original organ, there are significant differences.

In recent years there is a tendency to call these electronic organs by a more accurate name - **synthesizer**, and they do have the ability to emulate not only the organ, but any other instrument and beyond that to produce entirely new sounds, almost anything that the operator can imagine.   In the end, however, the sound emanates from speakers, and is therefore limited in subtle but very telling ways compared to a real pipe organ.

This can only be appreciated after hearing a pipe organ played expertly in its natural environment. Large organs are the work of master craftsmen who design and build the instrument specifically to fit a space and its architecture.   To build an organ was frequently an immense enterprise often involving years.   The results can be breathtaking to hear, to see, and even to feel - and we do feel a pipe organ.   To hear, in a large cathedral, the tremendous array of tones, subtones, overtones, and resultant tones emanating from a magnificent organ's many ranks of pipes is a unique, indescribable, and often, inspirational experience.

Organ

Harpsichord (English, 1781)

CHAPTER FOUR

The Orchestra

The Band

The term "band" is given to a great variety of ensembles. Until recently it applied to groups using mostly wind and percussion, without the stringed instruments found in the orchestra. In the medieval era roving bands of itinerant acrobats and jugglers wandered Europe from town to town, blowing and banging on wind and percussion instruments.

Larger and more organized military bands developed for marching and outdoor ceremonial affairs where the volume of winds and percussion was used to advantage. The traditional town band which could be found performing in town squares at the turn of the twentieth century also capitalized on the ability of wind instruments to be heard outdoors.   This was an important consideration in those times before electronic amplification was available.

Directly descended from both the town and military bands are the bands found in high schools and colleges in our own time.   Many of these bands continue to perform outdoors as "marching bands," in parades and at sporting events, and with somewhat modified instrumentation they also appear indoors as **concert bands**.

A smaller version of the concert band is the **wind ensemble**.   In addition to being smaller than the concert band, the wind ensemble uses less doubling of instruments. Players have more responsibility for their own parts, more like the demands of chamber music.

Bands are also found in jazz and rock music where the name applies freely to almost any group of players and singers: Dixieland, The Beatles, The Grateful Dead etc.   In the nineteen-forties, a somewhat more structured group was the jazz ensemble variously known as the big band, stage band or dance band, consisting of about fifteen to twenty players, usually saxophones, trumpets and trombones.   In the modern, rock music sense, a band has come to mean almost any group of performers.

The Orchestra Evolves

The distinction between band and orchestra hinges on the use, in the latter, of the violin family of instruments, violin, viola, 'cello and string bass. It was the perfection of these instruments in the seventeenth century that made the orchestra possible, the orchestra upon which so much of the great art music that followed would be profoundly dependent.

The orchestra is a wondrous creation. Like the most beautiful and miraculous works of nature, it is so much a part of life that we tend to take it for granted. Not only those who listen to art music are guilty. The orchestra is the voice of instrumental music. The truth of this can be found at the movies. Even in the newest films, after decades of domination by rock music, when we listen for the background music, we will most likely hear the orchestra.

From the most transparent tinkling of bells and delicate whispering of lush-voiced flutes, to the roar of the full orchestra with screaming brass and thundering timpani, the range of sounds is incredible. The orchestra is a phenomenon so elemental, so right in conception, that it could not have been invented. It is like a force of nature, a product of evolution, growing from some great natural plan. The instruments that are included have endured a "survival of the fittest" process.

For instance: The recorder was the preeminent wind instrument throughout the Baroque Period, but when the orchestra grew larger, around 1750, the recorder was replaced by the modern style transverse flute with its louder voice and wider dynamic range. The process is observable even today as the still more penetrating sound of the silver flute gradually replaces older style instruments made of wood. Today, only in some places in England and Germany do we still find the somewhat sweeter sounding but more muted older instrument.

The Modern Symphony Orchestra

The core of the orchestra is the string section. The strings have a unique sound when many players of the same instrument play the same part. This provides the heart of the orchestral sound - the characteristic string tone.

The strings of the orchestra are divided into five section: first violins, second violins, violas, 'cellos, and basses. The first violins are identical to the seconds in every way except that the composer writes separate parts for the two sections. The "firsts" generally have a higher part, usually the melody, and the "seconds" have a lower part.

The Baroque orchestra was usually a strings-only ensemble as winds and percussion were not yet routinely included. But even later on, when the standard orchestra did include the full compliment of winds and percussion, composers occasionally wrote for string orchestra.   To really hear the quality of string sound, choose one of these works, either from the Baroque or from later.   A good choice would be the *Serenade for strings in C* by Tchaikowsky. There is a unique vibrancy to the sound of

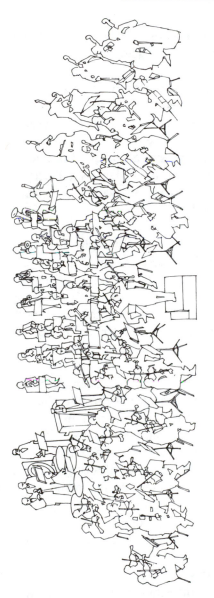

Symphony Orchestra

strings, an expansive richness; especially when the instruments are fine, old specimens.

In the best orchestras there is an active concern for the kind of instruments players use.   In the Philadelphia Orchestra, famous for the quality of string tone, if an orchestra member does not own a fine old Italian instrument, the orchestra arranges to provide one, supplied usually as a donation by a wealthy collector.   Remember, these instruments can be valued in the hundreds of thousands of dollars.

To complete the full symphony orchestra, winds and brass are added, usually in pairs (threes or fours if the orchestra is to be a very large one).   String players usually duplicate the same part - first violins all playing the first violin part, cellos all playing the cello part etc.   Wind players, on the other hand, are more like soloists in that each player is responsible for his or her own particular part.

Whereas a pianist or violinist can aspire to a solo career as a recitalist and concerto performer, there is less chance of a wind player making a career in this way.   For one thing the repertoire does not easily allow it.   The great composers wrote numerous masterpieces for violin and piano but there are only a handful of great works for winds, and even the best of these do not really compare with the Beethoven piano concertos, for instance.   Occasionally a wind player, through a combination of talent and personal charisma, can become famous and internationally acclaimed. The flutist James Galway is a current example, but this is highly unusual.   For wind players, a principal seat in a major orchestra is probably the height of attainable success.

Since there are usually three or four players of each wind instrument, the principal, or first chair player, is a sort of section leader and plays the higher, more prominent part. More importantly, the principal player is responsible for the exposed passages written for the instrument (called **solos**, after the Italian word for "alone"). The principal players in major orchestras are artist caliber performers with considerable reputations.

A digression: The author happens to be one of the few people in the world who does not appreciate football. This is no doubt because he has never learned what it is all about and it therefore appears to be two groups of men bumping into one another and falling down. However, one Thanksgiving the author's brother who was engrossed in a game on TV, pointed out that player number 12, on the team with the red and white suits, was one of the fastest men on earth, held world speed records etc.; and if his team could get the ball to him, he would run like the devil and nobody could catch him. It did not take much; with this information as incentive the author watched football with great enjoyment, just like a normal person.

Similarly, when attending an orchestral performance it can be helpful to be acquainted with the players. Phillip Meyers, for instance, plays Principal French horn in the New York Philharmonic (call him New York Phil). His playing is characterized by a wide expressive range, exuberance, and, great power. When the French horn has a solo and he is playing, you can be sure it will be heard, it will be interesting and it will be exciting. Of course, the more you come to know about the players, and about the conductor, the more interesting the performance will be. Among musicians and among non-musicians who are *enthusiastic fans, performers come to be well known and achieve a sort of celebrity. It is usually well deserved.*

With a few minutes of listening, the initiated listener can frequently tell which country an orchestra is from; national differences are readily apparent. It is not unusual for a good listener to name the exact group. To the new listener this may seem impossible, but there are many hints to the informed, perceptive ear. Orchestras have individual sounds and personalities, some known for the beauty of string quality and some for the power of the brass section. These things are not the most important aspects of becoming a successful listener, but they often make the process more interesting.

The Orchestra As A Cultural Force

We have examined the orchestra from a historical perspective and considered the orchestra as a sound generator. A third consideration is the orchestra as a centerpiece of modern cultural life. To rate as important, a city must support an orchestra; parallel, in a sense, to the way a professional sports team is desirable. It is the symphony orchestra that is the common measure of cultural life.

With the orchestra in place an entire season of art music can be sustained. Famous Maestros will fly in to conduct; internationally known soloists will make concerto appearances; large works like Handel's *Messiah* will be staged in conjunction with choral groups. In many cities the orchestra will also serve as the opera orchestra and play for dance companies in a ballet series.

Because of the nature of art music, orchestras rarely sustain themselves financially and require substantial fund-raising on their behalf. To be involved philanthropically in the support of an orchestra is a highly regarded effort in the most sophisticated circles. In the highest echelons of society it is important to be seen at the symphony. Some of these traditions raise questions of integrity that we have addressed. Is it honest and healthy to attend a performance for social rather than musical reasons? The point here, however, is that the orchestra is at the heart of an active, highly complex and compelling social phenomenon.

Rather than selling tickets to every concert as an individual project, the management of an orchestra concentrates on selling subscriptions, like season tickets. They are available in different types; a mini-series, for example, that might include a concert every two months, or a full series, including a concert every week. Advantages to the concertgoer are several: first, you will be sure that the concert will not be sold out; second, the more concerts are included, the more the price is discounted; third, the best seats are made available first to subscribers and then to single-concert sales.

For his music appreciation classes, the author always schedules an end of the semester trip to a concert at Lincoln Center. A peculiar and interesting reaction is expressed by a great many students. Being themselves in the audience and part of the crowd, they are somehow surprised that all of these people, thousands and thousands of them, partake of these events, that this goes on every night, that they are people in many ways much like the students themselves, and that many of them are really having a great time.

The Baroque Orchestra

The orchestra in the Baroque period was essentially a string group of about twelve to sixteen players plus harpsichord.   A bassoon was sometimes used to reenforce the 'cellos.   For large works composers added wind instruments usually in pairs, but in no standardized arrangement; horns, trumpets, oboes, flutes and timpani. Orchestration tended to reflect what the composer had available in the way of players.   Wind players were often required to play several instruments so that a composer such as J.S. Bach might call for two recorders in one movement and then expect the same two players to switch to oboes in another.   Some interesting instruments appear that became extinct after the Baroque period; the hauntingly beautiful oboe d'amore, for example, halfway between the modern oboe and English horn.

The Classical Orchestra

The orchestra grew to about thirty to forty players in the Classical period and winds were included as a standard feature.   The use of a harpsichord to play continuo parts gradually faded during this era.   The standard wind section included pairs of oboes and horns.   For larger orchestras, and more regularly toward the later Classical period, flutes, bassoons, trumpets and timpani were added. Clarinets made their first appearance in the orchestra at the end of the Classical era.

The Romantic Orchestra

The orchestra continued to grow during the Romantic period, reaching its ultimate modern day strength of approximately one hundred players.   More strings were added and brass and woodwinds grew from pairs to groups of three or four. Trombones and tuba completed the brass section.   Some extended forms of the regular woodwinds were added: the piccolo, soprano and bass clarinets, contra-bassoon and the English horn.   One or two harps were added if the composer wished.   The percussion section which had usually been limited to one player on timpani now grew to include three or more players switching back and forth to cover a huge array of percussion instruments; drums, cymbals, gongs, bells and numerous special sound effects.

Orchestration

How the composer assigns parts to the various instruments and the details of how the parts are arranged is called **orchestration**.   As the orchestra grew larger and more complex the process of orchestration became more demanding and required considerable study by composers to learn the ranges, abilities, strengths and limitations of the various instruments. Certain composers with a particular sensitivity to timbre raised orchestration to the level of an art; Berlioz, Rimsky-Korsakoff and Ravel are among them. The orchestral colors in Tchaikowsky's *Nutcracker* are phenomenal.

The Conductor

There is a certain skepticism among non-musicians about exactly what it is that a conductor does - this musician who makes no audible sound. Of course there is a lot of arm waving, gesticulating, and, in some conductors, dancing and jumping, but do these things really have an effect? Or, to put it another way, would not the orchestra play just as well without a conductor? To answer the question: Yes, it is possible for an orchestra to play without a conductor, but, in most cases, not just as well.

The art of conducting only dates back to the early Romantic period. Before that time conductors did not usually stand before the orchestra. Performances were rather "supervised," often by the composer, but from a position as player; either first violin, in which case he or she is called the **concertmaster,** or from the harpsichord. This practice has returned to an extent today in performances by ensembles specializing in early music. There are also **chamber orchestras** (small orchestras) that play without a conductor. The fact is, however, whether the conductor is standing or sitting, there are certain jobs that need to be accomplished.

When a jazz ensemble starts, the leader might say, "a-one, a-two, a-one two three four ... ," etc. This serves two main functions: It conveys the tempo and lets the players know when to begin. Art music requires the same things, but calling out numbers would poorly befit the situation. Tempo and starting point can be conveyed to the orchestra silently, through established conducting patterns. It is possible to assign this task to one of the players, but it can be clumsy to conduct and play at the same time and it is more difficult for all the players to see a seated leader. In short, it is usually not worth the effort to eliminate the conductor (although some hardened professional players, abused by dictatorial conductors would disagree with this sentiment).

There is also more to conducting than getting the ensemble going and at the right speed. Changes of tempo and dynamics that occur in the course of a work need to be indicated. Then there are innumerable aspects of interpretation to be dealt with. If every player went his or her own way on this, the result would be ragged, disjunct and probably cacophonous. It is the conductors job to decide matters of interpretation, from the smallest detail of articulation to the largest philosophical overview of the whole work and even the entire program (which the conductor usually chooses). The conductor must plan, organize and regulate the efficient running of rehearsals, allotting time to insure that the entire program is prepared for performance.

Orchestras usually have one permanent conductor, usually called the **Music Director,** and a number of guest conductors.   The permanent conductor is responsible for shaping some of the larger aspects of the orchestra, engaging players and choosing repertoire, things which affect the characteristic sound and distinguishing individual style of the ensemble.

The most important responsibility of the conductor, and the most elusive, is to focus the efforts of diverse individual musicians and to inspire them to a unified performance. This ability to inspire is what marks a conductor for greatness.   The legendary Arturo Toscanini (1867-1957) had this ability in the highest measure; the excitement and intensity of every player in the orchestra can be heard and felt in the extraordinary recordings that he made over his long career.

CHAPTER FIVE

Instrumental Forms

When we think of the dominant role played by the symphony orchestra in today's musical life, it may be hard to realize that purely instrumental music had a slow beginning and was overshadowed by vocal music until fairly recent history. In fact we often find the era before 1600 referred to as the "age of vocal music."

Historians gather information about the past largely from written and printed evidence. Almost all written music from the years before 1600 includes words along with the musical notation. At the same time, there appears to be an absence of printed instrumental music from these years. The logical conclusion is that music with words was intended to be sung. A closer look at the evidence, however, indicates that this was not entirely true.

The actual situation was more like this: Yes, most of this music was probably conceived for voices. But musicians from these early times had a much more open view of how music ought to be performed and were comfortable mixing voices and instruments together, or performing the same music with instruments instead of voices.   In these cases, in madrigals, for instance, where instruments performed some or all of the parts, the words were simply ignored by the players.

Early instruments were, in fact, more closely identified with the human voice.   Viols and recorders were built in sets, or **consorts**, as they were called, corresponding to the usual voice ranges of soprano, alto, tenor and bass.

Instrumentalists in pre-Baroque times were probably less like the highly specialized virtuosos of today's concert and orchestra scene, and more like our jazz musicians.   The similarity would extend to the preference for **improvisation** (making the music up spontaneously, rather than reading something previously composed and written down) which would explain the absence of much that we recognize as specifically instrumental, written music.   So while there may not have been a great deal of music written specifically for instruments, instruments were, nevertheless, certainly a part of everyday musical life.

Aside from substituting for voice parts, one of the main uses for instruments was to provide accompaniment for singing.   The lute, a cousin of the guitar, and keyboard instruments were especially well suited to this.

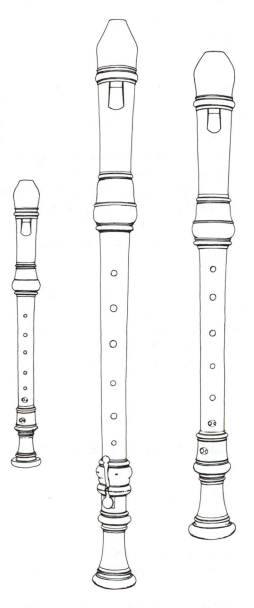

Instruments from a Consort of Recorders

Dance Forms

But when instruments were played without voices it was usually to provide music for dancing, and this has had a far reaching effect. You may encounter these dances - many of them originating in the Renaissance and Baroque periods - in performances by the increasing number of early music ensembles that play authentic instruments. In time, composers created extended, more complex or stylized versions of these dances, sometimes altering the original rhythmic structure and making them impractical for actual dancing. These versions served now as concert music, less functional, more artistic, and intended to be listened to rather than danced to.

Beginning in the Baroque Period, this phenomenon of dance-inspired concert pieces continues through the present day. The names of many early instrumental forms are the names of dances and indicate the character and, sometimes, the place of origin of the dance. Following is a listing of the more common of these:

Allemande: In moderate, duple time, from the Baroque period.

Bouree: From the Baroque period. Two fast beats per measure.

Courante: Lively, triple meter, usually including passages with rapid, running notes.

Galliard: 16th century, lively dance with high leaps. Triple meter from France. Considered risque at times.

Gavotte: Duple meter Baroque dance of a pastorale nature.

Gigue: (pronounced "zheeg"), related to the jig, compound meter, lively. Popular in the Baroque period.

Mazurka: Polish dance in lively, triple meter.

Minuet: Popular in the 1600 & 1700s. Moderate triple meter, often with a second section called a "trio."

Pavane: Stately, slow, duple meter 16th Century court dance.

Polonaise: Moderate, festive, processional dance from Poland.

Sarabande: From the Spanish Baroque, a slow, triple meter dance, usually with an accent on the second beat.

Siciliana: A languid, compound meter Baroque dance.

Movements

Large scale works are usually divided into independent, self contained sections called "**movements**." A twenty minute suite of dances, for instance, might include four movements of approximately five minutes each, some longer and some shorter. The end of a movement is usually marked by a final sounding cadence followed by a short, unmeasured pause before the next movement begins. In a live performance, audiences are expected not to applaud between movements.

Baroque Suite

The most obvious occurrence of these dance forms is in the Baroque suite, sometimes called Dance Suite. This is a fairly large scale, multi-movement work consisting of a series of stylized dances. Suites were usually written for harpsichord or orchestra. Bach wrote well known suites for violin alone, and even more unusual, 'cello alone. Standard movements in the suite are the allemande, courante, sarabande and gigue, establishing a slow-fast, slow-fast design. Into this basic structure could be inserted a choice of other dances. Larger suites often began with introductory movements; a prelude or an overture. An important characteristic of the suite is that all of the movements are in the same key. We will see that other large forms differ in this regard. Other names that were essentially interchangeable with "suite," at different times and places in the Baroque period, were partita, overture and sinfonia.

Formally, movements of the suite followed the particular rhythm, meter and character of the individual dances. They were often set up in **two part form,** each part repeated, A,A,B,B, with the A section modulating from tonic to dominant key, and the B section working back to the tonic. Alternately, movements appeared in **three part form** or ABA . This is the same pattern that we find in miniature in simple songs like *Twinkle Twinkle,* for instance, where "Up above the world so high, like a diamond in the sky" would be the "B" section. Elongated, to movement length, this elemental scheme is among the most frequently encountered forms in the Baroque Period and in other times as well.

Fugue

In discussing the fugue, or counterpoint in general, the term "Voice" will be encountered, even though, in most instances, the work is instrumental and not vocal. Voice, in this sense, refers to a limited range of pitches; comparable to the way human voices fall into soprano, alto, tenor, and bass ranges. We might speak about voices, as they relate to keyboard music, roughly as follows:

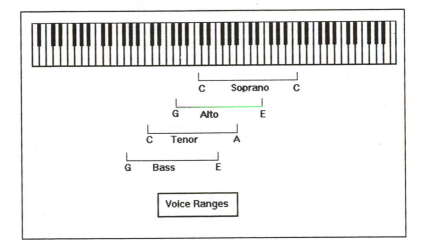

C Soprano C

G Alto E

C Tenor A

G Bass E

Voice Ranges

Fugues are among the best examples of polyphonic texture, and are highly imitative; that is, different parts or voices imitate one another in different ranges and pitch levels. Although fugues have been written by many composers right up to the present day, it is a form that is closely associated with the Baroque period.

The fugue is among the most highly structured of forms and, even to a beginning listener, usually recognizable. In simple terms, a fugue begins in one voice, (monophonic texture) with a statement of the main theme or **fugue subject** followed by other voices joining in with the subject in different voices and in different keys. It has the effect of an elaborate round (as when different singers or groups of singers perform Three Blind Mice, each beginning at a different pre-determined interval.)

The composer can treat the theme according to a number of contrapuntal devices, presenting it in versions that are longer, shorter, upside down, backwards, etc. Sections follow, called **episodes**, that may temporarily abandon the subject, but it returns periodically in further permutations.

The composition of a fugue is highly exacting and requires diligent study to master. The technical and mathematical aspects of this form may suggest that it could be a dry and bloodless form, but in the hands of a master musician such as the great J.S. Bach, the fugue can be exciting, expressive and uniquely satisfying.

Although they can be written for many musical media - piano, chorus, orchestra, etc.- fugues are strongly associated with the organ and a great many were composed for that instrument.

Forms Associated with the Organ

There are several other forms that, like the fugue, can be written for various combinations of instruments or voices, but are most closely associated with the organ, particularly in the Baroque period. Among these are the following:

Chaconne And Passacaglia

These terms were for the most part used interchangeably and indicate a form in which a series of bass notes are repeated throughout the piece, while above, the other voices form a series of melodic and harmonic variations that fit over the bass notes. The reiterating bass line provides unity while the variations in the higher parts supply variety.

Toccata

Literally, "touch piece," from the Italian. A composition, free in form, usually involving fast tempos and designed to exhibit the virtuosity of the player.

Fantasia

A freely structured piece in an improvisatory style. Found in the Baroque period frequently coupled with and preceding a fugue.

Concerto Grosso

Central to the concept of this orchestral form is the contrast and juxtaposition of a small group of instruments with a large group. The large group was the usual Baroque orchestra , called the **tutti**, meaning "all," or another term, **ripieno**. The small group, the **concertino**, was most commonly made up of two violins and a cello, although other instruments were sometimes used.

Concerti grossi (the plural form) were usually composed of three movements in a fast-slow-fast configuration and frequently developed around a device known as a **ritornello**, a theme of distinctive, easily remembered character, presented by the ripieno at the outset of the movement. The remainder of the movement consisted of contrasting sections played by the concertino alternating with recurrences of the ritornello. A final statement of the ritornello ended the movement.

Although it did not survive into the later style periods in its original form, the concerto grosso was highly important in the Baroque. Something about the contention between the large group and the small, made possible the natural extension of musical ideas over a longer span, creating a work of larger proportion and often greater effect. Highly important developments in the years following the Baroque era - the symphony and the solo concerto - grew directly out of the concerto grosso.

The Solo Concerto in the Baroque

In the Baroque era the solo concerto was very much related to the concerto grosso. In fact, we can think of it as a concerto grosso, in which the concertino is reduced from a small group to a single instrument. As in the concerto grosso, ritornello form served frequently as a basis for movements. Often, toward the end of a movement, the orchestra would be made to pause on an unresolved chord and the soloist would have an opportunity to spontaneously make up, or **improvise**, a passage based on the musical material of the movement while demonstrating impressive technical mastery of the instrument (**virtuosity**). These virtuosic improvisations were, in effect, extended cadences, thus called "**cadenzas.**"

When reference is made simply to "the concerto," most often what is meant is the solo concerto - a form more familiar to listeners because it survived through the Classical, Romantic and Modern eras - rather than the concerto grosso which essentially ended after the Baroque Period.

Basso Continuo

In considering any instrumental music of the Baroque Period, consideration must be given to a practice much akin to the constant presence of the rhythm section in jazz. A keyboard player (harpsichord or organ) and another instrumentalist playing a bass instrument (usually a 'cello or viola da gamba, but sometimes a bassoon or even a trombone), would serve as a unit. Composers wrote a **figured bass**, a bass part with figures below, which served as a shorthand to indicate the chord that should be played above the bass note.

The bass line would be played by the left hand of the keyboardist and doubled for reinforcement by the bass instrument. With the right hand, the keyboardist would fill in the indicated chords. There was considerable leeway in this system as to how the chords would be arranged or "voiced", and room for appropriate counterpoint. The keyboardist had to be well trained and able to meet the demands of the required improvisation.

This basso continuo was used as the basis for almost all music in the Baroque era, the exception being compositions for unaccompanied solo instrument.

Baroque Sonata

The Italian verb *Suonare*, meaning "to sound," tells us that a sonata is "to be sounded," or a "sound piece" (as a cantata is a piece to be sung). The Baroque sonata was written for a small group of instruments, usually from one to six. Some early sonatas were written in one movement with contrasting sections, but, in the later Baroque, the multi-movement sonata became the norm. Most commonly sonatas appeared in two types: trio sonata and solo sonata.

Chamber Music

The term **chamber music** is used to refer to non-orchestral instrumental music. It is naturally more intimate in character and includes from one to about a dozen players. These pieces were intended for performance in smaller settings. It can be difficult at times to distinguish between larger chamber works and small orchestra pieces, since a small Baroque orchestra requires only a dozen players. The important difference is that in orchestra, several players normally play the same part together as a section, whereas in chamber music, each performer plays his or her own part.

Trio Sonata

A highly popular form of chamber music in the Baroque period was the trio sonata, written for two solo instruments and basso continuo. Two flutes could be used, flute and violin, or any combination of instruments common to the period: flute, recorder, oboe and even the lower ranged 'cello and bassoon. Most common was a combination of two violins and continuo.

The name "trio sonata," can be confusing as there are actually four performers involved: two for the solo lines and two more to make up the basso continuo.

The fast-slow-fast arrangement of movements included a middle movement of flowing, songlike character and fast movements either dance inspired as in the Baroque suite or fugue-like, reflecting the contrapuntal character of this prominent Baroque phenomenon.

Although the trio sonata was by far the most common configuration for chamber music, other works were composed using the same forms and movements, but with different numbers of instruments. A Quartet, for instance, would consist of three instruments, each with an independent melodic line, and basso continuo. As with the trio sonata, the continuo is treated as a unit and we call the work a quartet even though five performers are required.

Baroque Solo Sonata

The Baroque period saw the rise of virtuosi, highly skilled instrumentalists capable of captivating audiences with expressiveness, tonal beauty and amazing technical display.   The solo sonata emerged, along with the solo concerto, as a vehicle for these talents.   In form the solo sonata reflected all the characteristics of the trio sonata but with one melody line rather than two above the basso continuo.

It should be noted that although the Baroque sonata developed directly into the sonata of the Classical period, substantial changes occurred that essentially redefined the form from about 1750 onward.

The Sonata And Sonata Form

A form developed in the Classical period that was to have a tremendous effect on the entire world of music.   It evolved as the first movement of the Classical sonata and is therefore called **sonata form**.   Distinguishing between the sonata and sonata form can cause communication problems, especially since sonata form can be found in many works that are not called sonatas.

Sonata Form

The three main sections of sonata form are the **exposition, development and recapitulation**. Essentially, as the names imply, thematic material is set out or exposed in the exposition section, developed in the development section and then recapped in the recapitulation.

To fully understand the greatness of this form, however, requires us to look at each of these sections in more detail. The first theme needs to be more than just a good melody. It is possible, for instance, to have a first theme that is in itself an excellent melody, but does not contain the potential for development; great composers could find themes that had both qualities. The theme is stated in the tonic, the home key of the work, and then followed by a second theme which should contrast both in character and in key. This change of tonality is usually accomplished through a **bridge** or **transition section**, appearing before the second theme and modulating from the tonic to the new key.

If the key of the piece is a major key, as is most often the case, the second theme will appear in the dominant key, establishing the elemental tonic-dominant relationship. If the work is in a minor key, the second theme will appear in the relative major key. (This change of mode is actually easier for most listeners to discern than the more subtle modulation from tonic to dominant).

A concluding section, sometimes involving a new **closing theme** or **codetta** ends the exposition with a cadence in the new key (the key of the second theme).

The modulation from key to key should be done smoothly, not abruptly, and, to the unsophisticated ear, may not be perceptible.   This shift, however, is thought to establish a subliminal tension, a subconscious feeling of wanting to return to the home key and a conflict between the two tonalities.   In the Classical Period the exposition section was usually repeated (this can confuse the inexperienced listener who may be expecting the development section to start).

It is from this conflict that the development section grows. Here, both the composer's imagination and skill are given full play. Thematic material from the exposition section returns, but in more complex configurations.   Themes are frequently sectionalized into fragments (**motives**); they may appear in a series of rapidly changing keys. Themes may be played against one another, stretched out, condensed, inverted or otherwise presented in altered states. Much goes on here that is reminiscent of techniques found in the fugue.

In the hands of a composer like Beethoven, the development process can remind the listener of nothing less than the course of a mighty battle.   Underlying all of this should be a sense of a working out of conflict. A feeling of arrival marks the return of the first theme, complete, in the home key (tonic).   This also signals the end of the development section and the beginning of the recapitulation. The recapitulation proceeds to bring back the themes in the original order.   Even in the last moments of the movement, however, we find a wonderful duality: the second theme appears just as it did in the exposition, but now it is in the home key; the same and yet different. Consequently, in place of the exposition section's conflict, we find a satisfying sense of fulfillment and arrival. A more complete closing section usually ends the movement, now called a **coda** (Italian for "tail"), as opposed to the diminutive "codetta" that ended the exposition section.

The opportunities inherent in this design for the balancing of tension and resolution, similarity and contrast, the expected and the surprise, are phenomenal.

Sonata form was arrived at through a gradual, evolution-like process involving many of the finest composers of the late Baroque and early Classical times. Notable among them were J. C. Bach (son of the great J. S. Bach), Joseph Haydn and, of course, the great W. A. Mozart, who brought the form to its characteristic perfection. Sonata form satisfied the need for a vehicle to extend musical thoughts, creating movements of increased length, complexity and depth. The capacity of this form to sustain the most profound ideas of the great musical minds was close to miraculous. No wonder then, that since its advent not only the sonata, but movements in almost all symphonies, concertos, overtures and many other works follow this extraordinary form.

Since this form evolved as the first movement of the classical sonata it is alternately known by two other names: **first movement form** and, because the first movement of the sonata was usually marked "allegro" (fast in Italian), **Sonata Allegro form**.

In the classical period works that were called sonatas were essentially solo sonatas. Many were written for piano alone, which replaced the harpsichord as the main keyboard instrument of the time. Sonatas were also written for other instruments, most often the violin. In these cases, where the sonata was written for an essentially one-note-at-a-time instrument, accompaniment would be provided by the piano, which had replaced the basso continuo of the Baroque era for this purpose.

The repertoire of the Classical period includes many sonatas, particularly those of Haydn and Mozart for piano and for violin, of masterpiece quality. These composers found in this form a vehicle that was attractive and satisfying to both the performer and the listener and was, at the same time, able to carry the weight of real expression for those who were willing and able to look deeper.

The Sonata Cycle

So far we have had a look at the form that evolved in the first movement of the Classical sonata. The sonata, however, included three individual movements, usually in fast-slow-fast order. Although either or both of these later two movements could and sometimes did appear in sonata form, other forms of the era were commonly used.

Most common among these were the following:

• Three part or ABA form.

• Theme and variations. As the name implies, this form consists of a theme, either original or borrowed, followed by a series of variations based on the theme.

• Rondo. This form, usually in a quick tempo and most often found as the last movement of a multi-movement work, is characterized by a catchy main theme that recurs frequently throughout the piece.

We have seen that a change of key played an important role within sonata form. Key change was also a factor between movements. The first movement would, of course, be in the home key of the work; a composition called *Sonata in C Major*, for example, would have a first movement in C major. The second movement would be in a related but different key, often the dominant or subdominant and the last movement would return to the original key. You will notice a reflection here, but on a larger scale, of the key scheme of the sonata form found within the first movement.

A number of other highly important forms of the Classical era and later were, in a sense, members of the sonata family. The symphony and the concerto are among these. The symphony can be thought of as a sonata written for orchestra, a concerto as a sonata for solo instrument and orchestra. Another form, the overture, was in most cases identical in structure to the first movement of a symphony.

String Quartet

By far the most important chamber music ensemble was the string quartet. This combination of two violins, viola and cello provided the ideal vehicle to inspire composers to new heights of expression. Because the quartets were often intended for performance by the composers themselves together with their colleagues (often other composers), the works were carefully crafted and tended to convey more personal ideas than did the larger, more public works.

Like its larger relative, the symphony, the string quartet was addressed by almost all of the important composers of the nineteenth and twentieth centuries.   The list of outstanding contributors to the literature for quartet includes Haydn, Mozart, Beethoven, Schubert, and in the twentieth century, the Hungarian composer Bela Bartok.

String Quartet

The late quartets of Beethoven merit special mention. Written in the composer's last years when deafness had completely overtaken him, they stand alone as works of transcendental character.   These quartets offer the supreme challenge to those listeners who are in pursuit of the highest and most compelling levels of music.

The Sonata in Other Chamber Works

From the Classical period on there appeared a broad range of chamber works, larger and smaller than the string quartet, that were likewise constructed around the sonata cycle; duos, trios quintets etc.   In effect, any example of chamber music was a sonata for instrumental ensemble.   The first movement would appear in sonata form and the usual order of movements would follow, as in the symphony and solo sonata.   Most used string instruments and some called for various mixed combinations of piano, strings and winds.   Generally, names for these chamber works reflect the status of the string quartet as the basic unit. Therefore, a work for piano and string quartet would be called a piano quintet; a work for French horn and string quartet would be a horn quintet.   A work for violin, viola, cello and horn would be called a horn quartet based on the idea that the horn serves in place of one of the violins of the normal string quartet.

Fortunately, today, excellent performances of chamber music are available for the interested listener.   Chamber works provide a very different kind of musical experience than orchestral works or opera.   In place of a powerful mass of sound and varied colors, chamber music offers the opportunity to be close, physically and musically, to a small ensemble, usually made up of some of the finest players of the time.   Among musicians, the best chamber players may be considered a step above orchestral musicians, as the demands are for sensitivity and intellect along with excellent technical ability.   Chamber music does not usually appeal to mass audiences the way larger forms do.   It attracts a smaller, elite audience.   But for those listeners with the capacity to fathom the expressive depths of this intimate medium, the rewards are great.

The Symphony

The Baroque period had provided the first large scale works for orchestra in the dance suite and the concerto grosso. The Classical period would see the influence of these works blossom in a new form, a kind of sonata for orchestra, which became known as the **symphony**.

In the Baroque dance suite it had been a common practice to insert a popular, less formal dance before the last movement. This tradition carried over to the symphony. Into the basic three movements, fast-slow-fast, was inserted a minuet, a courtly dance in a moderate triple meter, that was popular in the period. Placed after the slow movement and before the **finale** (concluding movement) it provided a change of mood. The symphony was developing into a substantial form, and often included deeper and more serious moods. The minuet served much like comic relief in drama to lighten the tone after what might have been a highly expressive or dramatic slow movement.

With its four movement pattern the symphony attracted the best efforts of the composers of the Classical age. As with the sonata, the symphonies of Haydn and Mozart are among the great treasures of music. The "London" symphonies, written at the end of Haydn's output of more than 100 symphonies, are among his best works in the form. Mozart composed 41 symphonies in his short 35 year existence, and the last three of these, Numbers 39, 40, and 41 ("*The Jupiter*"), are unsurpassed.

Beethoven and the Symphony

Beethoven's nine symphonies are arguably the greatest set of pieces ever created. He took the symphonic form from Haydn and Mozart and infused it with outward expressions of the joy and sadness of life. He also had the unique ability to create inspiring passages that we all recognize as tonal representations of a great, heroic striving. This unique characteristic of Beethoven was unheard of up to that time and remains unequalled since. With Beethoven symphonies grew longer and the orchestration grew larger. He called for more strings than his Classical forebears and added trombones and contra-bassoon. He replaced the minuet with the scherzo, still in triple meter but faster and more exuberant. The Beethoven symphonies are the heart of any orchestra's repertoire; they are known and loved by more listeners than any other body of works. Like the plays of Shakespeare, they are monumental. They are among the first and the last works any serious listener should experience.

The Symphony Beyond Beethoven

Since Beethoven, the symphony has been of central importance in the work of serious composers. Only a handful have escaped the challenge of composing symphonies: Chopin, who specialized in piano music, and some (Verdi and Wagner for example) who consciously limited their work to the field of opera. The list of those who made significant contributions to symphonic literature is long and distinguished.

In the late Romantic period, composers reserved their finest efforts for the challenges of symphonic composition, with

Brahms and Tchaikowsky each composing some of their most important works in this genre. Even in the twentieth century, with its rejection of and disdain for tradition, the symphony retains a role of central importance with landmark works such as those of Gustav Mahler and Dmitri Shostakovich. To credit the symphony with its full measure of influence, consideration must also be afforded the many works in the late Romantic and Contemporary eras that, while they may have different names, are either symphonies in disguise or very heavily influenced by the symphony. The list of these works would be a long one.

For well over two centuries now symphonies have been the main artery through which composers communicate their best, their most deeply felt and most carefully expressed thoughts to the world. Newcomers to music usually find symphonies a satisfying starting point. Listeners are free to interpret the abstract sounds in any way that works for them. The balance in structure of the forms and movements has proven uniquely satisfying and able to bear multiple levels of expression. The sonic glory of the orchestra adds the dimension of color inherent in the many combinations of instrumental timbre, while the combined forces can thrill the listener to heights of ecstasy through sheer sonic power. The symphonic embodiment of form through orchestral sound is certainly among the highest achievements of art, nature and the human spirit.

The Concerto

The concerto, like the symphony, came together as a form in the Classical period. As to origins, it is a complex and interesting phenomenon. On the one hand, it may be thought of as a version of the sonata cycle, parallel to the symphony, but scored for solo instrument and orchestra. On the other hand, it clearly derives from the Baroque concerto grosso by way of the Baroque solo concerto. Evidence of both lines of ancestry can be found in the form. A version of sonata form can usually be discerned in the first movement - with a twist. The twist is called a double exposition whereby the exposition is presented by the orchestra (this would appear for the most part indistinguishable from the first section of a typical symphony) followed by a repeat of the exposition, but this time with the solo instrument taking a leading role.

From another point of view, we can very often find clear elements of the ritornello form of Baroque concertos; much more so than appear in symphonies. The result is often an interesting hybrid form. For those listeners who enjoy analytic listening, the complex configurations of concerto form can be intriguing. (An essay by the eminent writer on music, Sir Donald Francis Tovey, on Mozart's C major Piano Concerto K.# 503 provides a fascinating, classic study of this subject.)

A particular feature of concerto form is the cadenza, found toward the end of the first movement and occasionally in other movements as well. The orchestra suspends an unresolved chord and the soloist, unaccompanied, embarks on a passage, based on the work's main themes. Lasting anywhere from a few seconds to several minutes the cadenza is designed to exhibit unusual and impressive virtuosity.   In the Baroque period, where this convention began, cadenzas were improvised on the spot by the soloists. This remained true through the classical period, but by the Romantic age composers tended to provide written out cadenzas rather than leave this to the soloist. There are concertos written for cello, clarinet, all the usual orchestral instruments - and even some for very unusual, non orchestral instruments.

The most numerous and most famous concertos, however, are written for the main instruments of art music; piano and violin.

Highly reminiscent of the Baroque concerto grosso are a number of more unusual concertos for more than one solo instrument. Brahms wrote a Double Concerto for violin and cello and Beethoven, a Triple Concerto for violin, 'cello and piano, as solo instruments.

For those in the beginning stages of an involvement with art music the concerto has a special appeal. This is true for the same reasons that concertos are widely popular with audiences. The concerto is a particularly engaging kind of work to listen to because it combines the great tonal resources of the orchestra with the fascinating display of solo virtuosity.

It is important to recognize that orchestra concerts are the most frequent and substantial facet of musical life in the Western world. All but those who live in the most remote and isolated regions have access to orchestra programs, either major orchestras in cities, one of the many regional orchestras or touring orchestras.

The conductors who put together programs for the orchestras are aware that famous soloists who are well known through their recordings are very attractive to audiences, and it is a rare orchestra program that does not include a concerto. The concerto typically enjoys the coveted place on the program right after intermission because this is what many listeners wait for with great anticipation.

To appear as soloist in a concerto performance with a great orchestra is the ultimate goal of every serious instrumentalist. Those few who succeed in reaching this goal endure years of the most intense training and long hours of constant and sustained practice.   They need brilliant talent coupled with a fierce competitive spirit.   Those who survive the challenge and secure an engagement to perform a concerto have the power to fascinate and to thrill audiences.

It is a difficult fact of a soloist's life that he or she must be on the road a great deal, traveling from one country and city to the next.   But this provides one of the great aspects of our modern concert life: People all over the Western world have the opportunity to see and hear these conjurors with sound in live performance and to learn first hand that the superstar status of famous concerto performers is earned by those who can not only dazzle an audience, but who can move the listener to great heights of emotion.

CHAPTER SIX

Opera

Opera is a play set to music, staged and acted, with costumes and scenery. The dialogue is sung, accompanied by orchestra. It is, at the same time, the most hated and most loved of art forms.

Those who object to opera usually cite three very compelling reasons:

1. People do not usually sing to one another. It is artificial and unrealistic, therefore hard to accept.

2. Opera is usually sung in a foreign language so it is impossible to tell what's going on. Reading the plot of the story while listening is tedious and in a live performance they always turn down the lights so you can't read anyway.

3. The voices are too loud and emotional. It sounds like a lot of screeching and screaming.

To answer these complaints requires an understanding of the essential nature of opera.

Suppose that you are waiting in line to get in to the 9:30 showing of a new movie. You see someone you know coming out of the 7:20 showing. You exchange greetings and ask if they liked the movie. "Oh, it was great," your friend says, "especially at the end when E.T. comes back to life." What is your reaction? You are ready to kill your friend. Now you know what happens at the end! The movie is ruined!

The main job of a movie is to tell a story. Opera is different. The main job of opera is to convey the emotional consequence of a story. It may be the feeling of terror when a murderer steps out of the shadows; we hear it as a frightened shiver in the orchestra. It may be an enslaved people finding the will to oppose a cruel oppressor; we hear it as mighty voices raised together in a courageous, thrilling chorus. It may be a young woman's grief at the death of a lover, sung to a heart-rending melodic line overflowing with sadness.

In each case, the important thing is that opera goes beyond the event and conveys to us the feeling behind it. Opera recounts a story, but with a fourth, added dimension; beyond the words and actions we find emotions made manifest, expressed, revealed in the music; revealed to hear with our ears and to feel in our hearts. When it works it provides a most powerful, most exhilarating, most moving experience.

This is not to say that the story is unimportant. Taken by themselves, the emotions expressed in opera can be found in abstract form in instrumental music. The great thing about opera is the *connection* between the story and the music. It *is* therefore of great importance to know what is happening. This is a problem if the opera is presented in a foreign language. A lively debate had been going on about the wisdom of translating opera into the local language. This was done, rarely in the United States, but more frequently in Europe. An Italian opera, for example, presented in Germany would be translated and sung in German.

Those against this practice pointed out that the text of an opera is usually in verse; that the composer sets poetry to music. Even the best and most carefully done translation will not place the music with the language the way the composer did originally. Rhymes and the particular sounds of the language, where the consonants and vowels fall in relation to the notes, how the important words and syllables fall on stressed notes, how the natural rhythm of the language is reflected in the music, all would be destroyed in translation. They added that even if you did the translation, the truth is that listeners do not really understand words when they are sung anyway. Why not leave the opera in the original language where, at least, it will sound best?

Those in favor of translation admitted that these were compromises, but they insisted that it was completely ludicrous and against the composer's wishes to have the audience unable to understand the language. Who cared if the stress fell on the right word if the listener did not know what the word meant?

And so the debate raged for years. Fortunately, we live in a time when the controversy has been largely resolved. For about ten years now in the United States, many opera companies present operas sung in the original language but with an English translation projected in foot high letters, called supertitles, above the stage. At first it may seem annoying to have to glance up to read the translation. But just as with subtitles in foreign films, after a short time the process becomes largely subconscious, automatic, and we understand what is being sung. This wonderful innovation has allowed a tremendous advance in making opera accessible and enjoyable to millions. The only bad news is that some of the more conservative opera companies have resisted using supertitles. The Metropolitan Opera in New York, where many of the finest productions and the greatest singers in the world appear is, unfortunately, at the time of this writing, among them.

We do not criticize sculpture because it does not move. Sculpture is not intended to move. Opera is not intended to be realistic, not in a literal sense. When we watch TV we accept many conventions. People sit around three sides of a table to leave a convenient angle for the camera and they never seem to need to go to the bathroom. In a play, we accept that the house on the set has only three walls. We accept sung dialogue in musicals because we are accustomed to this convention. In a sense, all songs are musical speech and we accept this because we are accustomed to do so. We are disturbed by the convention of singing in opera because it is unfamiliar to us. The solution is to become accustomed to the convention of sung drama, in essence to outgrow the problem like millions before have done, to their great enrichment, for four centuries now.

Have you ever had the experience of seeing a pop singer on TV, smiling and grooving along, but when you really listen you notice that the words are about something very sad? "Why is this person acting so mellow when his 'Baby up and left him'? ," you ask. This usually does not happen, by the way, with the very best pop singers, who do express the meaning of the words.

Like the best of the pop artists, good opera definitely reflects the meaning of the words, and herein lies a problem, but only for those who are not aware of what is being sung about. Where many songs might be about small, everyday feelings and events, someone feeling blue or missing someone, or needing to dance, dance, dance, opera tends to deal with larger, deeper feelings and events. Like the plays upon which most operas are based, they commonly involve matters of life and death; strong emotions result.

Suppose you are flipping channels on the TV to see what is on. Between toothpaste commercials, baseball games, cartoons, etc. you happen to pause on NET. You see a woman singing in Italian with great emotion and great volume. Under the circumstances your reaction might be, "What is this woman's problem?" Well may you ask.

The opera is "_Il Trovatore_," and the singer is the gypsy Adeljesa. She is reliving the night her infant son was torn from her and thrown to a death by fire. Yes, her voice is strained, but when we know why, we see that it is appropriate and understandable. Rather than seeming over-done, when we are involved, it holds us in a powerful grasp. Madonna sings about problems too, but they are usually of a different kind and require a different approach.

Operas last an entire evening; opera is a large-scale form and reaches dramatic heights impossible to attain in a two minute song. Opera is emotional. That is why, when given a chance, it grips listeners with an intensity impossible to equal, except by life itself.

The Operatic Voice

By its very nature opera demands to be done in a large hall. It is large scale: Orchestra, chorus, principal singers (usually very highly paid), costumes, sets, stagehands, etc.. To pay the bill for opera it is necessary to sell many tickets and provide enough seating. This requirement, to present opera in a large hall, has had an important effect on the nature of operatic singing. Until the middle of the twentieth century electronic amplification was not available. The ability to project the voice and be heard by large audiences quickly became an important requirement for successful opera singers.

This kind of large voice and projected sound, in addition to the ability to be heard, carried an important dividend. It had a quality that could be ravishingly beautiful. Something about producing the great volume of sound required, invested the voice with a special strength, an urgency, striking in its ability to affect the listener; something intensely visceral. Taking a voice of less than operatic size and amplifying it does not provide anything like the same effect. The right sound can only be achieved the old fashioned way, through long training, intense practice and real physical effort.

It is for this reason that even today, when we have the technology to amplify voices, microphones are never found in the opera house. A singer of opera takes pride in the ability to be heard. Using a microphone would be highly demeaning. When you go to the opera to hear Pavorotti, wherever you sit, you hear him direct, no electricity involved, person to person. Only when you experience this live will you understand the real significance of it.

The range of the voice became important as well. Composers tended to stretch limits of the normal voice and called for the ability to sing extremely high and in some cases extremely low. This forcing of the voice into what for most humans would be highly unnatural registers also had the effect of heightening the urgency of sound.

Opera singing became highly selective. Not only were talent and dedication called for, but now the requirement was to possess a voice of unusual natural size and one that could be trained to negotiate the extended registers. It is very similar to professional basketball. You may be a superlative athlete, quick and smart; but if you are short, can you really hope to play with the big guys? Not very democratic, but such are the demands of the game; the same with opera.

When we go to the opera house, therefore, we hear phenomenal voices. To reach this level the singers must have met all the requirements. They must be highly trained, skilled musicians, fine actors, their voices must be capable of great range and great power and, of course, the voice must have another important but intangible attribute: It must be beautiful to listen to.

All of this has consequences, some good and some bad. The good is that when we hear operatic singing at its best, it is incomparable. The sound of Enrico Caruso opening up his huge voice and thundering a high B flat or C is one of the most awesome and thrilling sounds imaginable. The bad is that when it is not good, like the little girl with the curl, it can be horrid.

Getting to the top in the professional world of opera is highly demanding and highly competitive. It requires that the singer be possessed of a rare voice and beyond that, rigorous training, excellent conditioning, great determination and an element of good luck.. This does not always happen early. It may take many years before an aspiring singer gets a chance to prove him or herself in a major role, and then more years to gain critical acclaim and finally recognition and fame. The demands of the climb to the top (keep in mind the extreme demands this kind of singing makes) have more than once ruined a voice.

It is a sad and ironic fact that often by the time a singer has gained the fame required to be frequently before the public, the voice is either damaged or aging. It is a rare opera singer that will give up the rewards of fame, however, and we frequently find these singers to be very active. A great singer in his or her prime is a glorious thing to behold, but, pushed past that time, it can be excruciating to hear; it is not in the nature of opera singers to be cautious or to hold back. It is highly unfortunate that much of what is presented as opera is done by singers relying on past reputations and who are no longer adequate to the task. The highly negative impression that a great many people have of opera singing comes from this all too common phenomenon.

The author remembers hearing an aging singer of great fame, Zinka Milanov. She had a huge voice, but had developed the large wobble in the sound that characterizes many spent older sopranos. The effect was so ridiculous and memorable that when we got a new kitten with a loud but very obnoxious meow we named her after the singer. It was years later that we heard recordings of Milanov in her prime. It was the most meltingly beautiful singing, characterized by exquisite taste and, ironically, the most absolutely elegant control of every nuance. Zinka Milanov, our cat, has been a constant reminder of the danger of being too quick to judge.

Going To The Opera, A How-To Guide

Of course you do not have to actually go to the opera. You can find excellent recordings that will yield great satisfaction. But if you do not actually attend the opera you will not fully experience it. Opera is after all a theatrical medium and the live experience is what you should pursue. But don't just buy a ticket and go.

1. Choose an opera. Mounting an opera is a huge commitment and opera companies tend to be very conservative, all presenting the same relatively small number of operas season after season. The operas that are performed represent a small percentage of the operas that were written. If an opera does not succeed initially it does

not get into the "repertoire." There have probably been many injustices done through the years and there may be many wonderful operas that lie neglected. It is often pointed out that the opera *Carmen,* one of the most universally loved operas in the world, was not initially greeted with the acclaim that it has since won. The composer, George Bizet, who had exhausted his considerable genius in creating this masterpiece, was terribly demoralized by the lack of recognition and within three months of the premier performance, his spirit crushed, he died at the age of thirty-seven.

The process that gives us the limited repertoire that survives comes under regular criticism. Cries are heard that opera companies should be more adventurous in giving more works, old and especially new. No doubt this is true, but for our purposes it is important to realize that the standard repertoire is highly select - sifted by time; the works that remain are of proven high quality and greatly loved by millions. You are safe in choosing almost any of these works.

Determine what opera will be given that you can attend. Although the repertoire is not huge, it still includes more works than you will ever be able to listen to. Opera companies rehearse a small selection of these each year and cycle them repeatedly throughout the season. You cannot assume that every opera will be available every year, even in the largest cities.

Having determined what is available, buy the best ticket you can afford for a performance at least six weeks in the future. Remember that opera houses tend to be very large. When the time comes to attend the opera you will be very glad that you have a good seat rather than being stuck up in the rafters where you can barely see the singers. Try for a well known opera by Verdi or Puccini if you have a choice. These are in the best, mainline Romantic Italian tradition and will guarantee a highly memorable experience.

Next, find a recording of the opera; CDs are best. You may find it in the library or you may buy it. (See Chapter Eleven for help with this.)   Opera recordings can be expensive as they require two or three CDs. You will be investing a great deal of time and energy in this opera so you will be glad to have the recording. You will probably want to return to it many times in the future.

The goal now is to become familiar with the music. A good plan would be to have listened to the entire opera five or six times before the live performance.   Operas are arranged in acts, most operas having three or four acts. Start with the first act and listen through a few times casually. The idea is to begin to develop a familiarity. This can be done while you are doing other things, without giving complete attention. In keeping with the guidelines established in Chapter One, resist making any judgement about the piece at this point.

After several sessions the music will begin to sound familiar, especially certain parts. At this point consult the **libretto** that is almost always included with recordings. The libretto is the text of the opera. This will usually include an act-by-act summary of the story and then the entire text in two side-by-side columns: the original language and the translation.

You will notice that some sections are speech-like, called **recitative**, and some sections are more song-like; these are **arias**. In the recitative sections, the story is advanced; we find out what is happening, what they are saying. In the aria sections we find out how they feel about it. The recitatives will tend to be more like prose and the arias like poetry. Study the words of the aria as you would a poem, then listen to the music and carefully follow the words. Notice how the composer has reflected the meaning of the text, not just generally, but line by line and even word by word. This contemplation of the relation between the poetry and the music is an intellectual challenge requiring real thought, but the results are almost always highly satisfying and well worth the effort. By now you will begin to find some sections particularly beautiful, melodic, or affecting. Make an effort to remember the first few words. This is how we refer to the various sections, usually arias, and will be useful in reading about or discussing the opera.

Repeat this process with the remaining acts, one by one. A word of caution: When you get to know one act you will have a tendency to want to listen to that act over again. When you start the next act you will not like it as much. Be strong! Push on! Resist the tendency to get stuck on Act One.

You will find that you have parts that you like and parts that you do not. Some of the parts that are not interesting will become more interesting as you get to know the opera. You will be amazed that some of your favorite parts went entirely unnoticed the first few times through. This is a characteristic of great music: the listener continues to find new levels - it is ever-changing.

When you have finished this process you should have listened to each act approximately four or five times. Now read whatever you have available in the way of information about the opera. Recordings usually come with considerable written material of this sort. If not, check the library for one of the many books that provide information on specific operas. At this point, reserve several hours, make yourself comfortable and go right through the opera, carefully following the libretto. You already know the story, but you will find that living through it start-to-finish, may provide a compelling continuity.

This should prepare you for the live performance. You probably found that the recording provided an experience of some force. You will probably not be prepared for how much more powerful the live performance will be. Because it is music, opera is essentially a sound centered phenomenon, but it is also very much a multidimensional combination: music, literature and theater - theater, of course, calling upon the visual arts. When it all comes together, the effect can be transcendental.

Opera is expensive; it is by nature grand, extravagant and sumptuous. Now, with lighting, scenery, visible action, physical interaction between characters, the magic of live theater, you will understand how opera has enthralled and uplifted those who have found it, for centuries.

Be prepared for some surprises. Your recording was always the same, without errors. The live performance may not be. Opera is preeminently demanding, requiring of singers the ultimate in skill, concentration and stamina. There is an excitement about anticipating a difficult, spectacular passage or climactic high note. Some of what you hear at the live performance will not be as perfect as the recording, but some of it will be better. The excitement, the immediacy of a live performance can inspire singers to phenomenal heights, thrilling to experience.

The author recalls a live performance of Puccini's Turandot at the Metropolitan Opera with the powerful but inconsistent tenor Franco Corelli as Calaf, the Prince. This particular evening Corelli was in magnificent voice; he could do no wrong. At the end of his famous aria, Nessun Dorma, Calaf determines to answer three riddles proposed by the Princess Turandot, with death as the consequence of failure. The score calls for the tenor to finish the aria and then mount a long set of stairs to ring a gong summoning the Princess. As Corelli finished the aria, his final climactic note rang out with tremendous force; and then, as he ran up the stairs still singing, the note began, unbelievably, to grow in intensity until the entire building seemed to vibrate. The ovation of the shocked and thrilled audience was overwhelming. A moment like that could only happen at a live performance.

To create great opera requires a composer with a very special gift. Wonderful melodies, harmonies and satisfying forms are important as they are in all of music, but beyond these things, the measure of an opera composer is the ability to capture feelings as expressed in words and actions and to translate these directly into music. Two composers who excelled above all others in this capacity and are therefore the greatest of opera composers, are Mozart and Verdi. They combined a sensitivity to understand the emotions attending the human condition and the genius to distill and illuminate these feelings through music in infinite array.

Arias involve one of the characters singing alone. Other often very interesting sections involve several singers together.   These sections, called ensembles, can include from two to as many as six different characters singing at the same time.   An ensemble for two is called a duet - as you might expect, love duets are very common.   Larger ensembles are called, in order, trios, quartets, quintets and sextets.   (There are also times when the stage will be full of a great number of singers, but these are choruses, in which many singers duplicate parts.)

The greatest opera composers have the mysterious ability to compose an ensemble that makes complete sense as a whole, and yet, if we focus on any of the individual singers, we will hear that his specific part perfectly expresses his own very subjective point of view.   This aspect of opera can engage the wonder of even the most advanced and experienced listener.

In your trip to the opera house you may encounter individuals who will be recognizable as opera fans.   A word about this unique breed of individual is probably in order. They are crazy for opera.   There is no real way to predict who will be infected by this virulent addiction. They come from all walks of life, business people, professionals, cab drivers, gym teachers and some who appear to be borderline derelicts.   They have found something very special at the opera house, something that brings them back as often as they can afford to come; a kind of vibrant super-life.   Is there a genetic tendency at work here or is it contagious? Are you susceptible?   The only way to find out is to get involved.   ...Or you could take up bowling.

CHAPTER SEVEN

Voices

For solo singing in art music we traditionally divide voices into six main types. In order from highest to lowest they are: Soprano, mezzo-soprano, alto, tenor, baritone and bass.

Soprano is the high female voice. In operatic singing different types of soprano are called for: **Dramatic sopranos** have a large sound capable of conveying powerful emotions. **Coloratura sopranos** have highly flexible voices effective in fast runs and trills (the rapid alternation of two consecutive notes).

Mezzo soprano is the mid-range female voice. This voice may be difficult to distinguish from the soprano as professional mezzos can attain extremely high tones. The difference can be in the weight and color of the voice as well as in range. The role of *Carmen*, in the opera of the same name is a famous mezzo-soprano role.

Contralto is the low female voice.   Here again the color of the voice differs from the soprano, being deeper and darker.   Voice teachers are constantly on the lookout for examples of the true contralto voice which they maintain is a rare and wonderful thing.

Tenor is the high male voice.   In discussing the tenor voice we encounter an interesting phenomenon.   Men generally have two separate kinds of voices: the **head voice** and the **chest voice**.   The chest voice is the normal, lower male voice and the head voice is the somewhat strange sounding high voice, otherwise known as falsetto.   This is the voice a man would use to imitate a little girl or to talk like Mickey Mouse.   Yodelling is the switching back and forth from head voice to chest voice.   It is possible, and fairly easy to sing the notes at the top of the tenor range in head voice.   The switch from chest to head is difficult to negotiate smoothly and the head voice has a floating, very light quality.   Some tenors who cultivate a light sound do use the head voice for high notes.   Other tenors would never consider it, and use the chest voice all the way to the highest notes.   These are the operatic tenors with heroic, trumpet-like voices.   While the chest voice is much more powerful, it is more difficult to produce and sustain and is far more apt to break, which is disastrous on stage.

Baritone is the medium male voice midway between tenor and bass.

Bass is the low male voice.   As you might imagine, the bass voice is darker and heavier than the tenor.   Differences between baritone and bass can be very small, and it is fairly common to find singers labeled **bass-baritone**, indicating that they can sing either part.

The author, who is a very poor, strictly amateur singer, claims to be a bass-baritone. In this case, what this means is that bass parts are too low and baritone parts are too high.

A basso profundo is a bass capable of singing very low notes. Lower notes are by nature much more difficult to project over an opera orchestra, and require a bass voice of huge, booming capacity. A **Basso** (the commonly used Italian word for bass) with a wonderful dark, dense quality is called a "black bass."

Voice Types in Choral Music

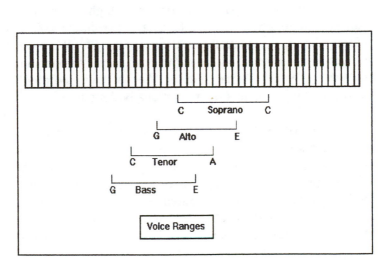

In music written for chorus or choir, the middle range voices, mezzo-soprano and baritone, are ignored and only four categories are traditionally recognized: Soprano, alto, tenor and bass - although if the composer wants more than four parts, these can be subdivided; sopranos into sopranos I and sopranos II, etc.

Some Unusual Voice Types

Castrato

Some background is required to understand this rather bizarre phenomenon. Before the sixteenth century religious and social strictures prevented women from appearing in public as singers. Similar conventions held for acting; for instance, and women in the Shakespeare plays were played by male actors specializing in female roles. Since women were not available for public performance, high chorus and solo parts were given to boys to sing. The boy's voice, before puberty, is essentially in a soprano range. We have vestiges of this practice in the many boys choirs throughout the Western World. Some, like the Vienna Boys Choir and the Harlem Boys Choir, are internationally famous.

The change to the mature, lower male voice begins at somewhere around the age of thirteen. It was the practice in past centuries to preserve a promising young singers high voice by surgically removing the sex organs before puberty. Putting aside the social consequences, this resulted, ultimately, in an individual of full male size, or as a result of the procedure, somewhat larger than ordinary size, and a high soprano or alto voice. These individuals were called castrati, were given rigorous training, and reportedly developed beautiful voices of high range, but with a subtly different quality. *The author has heard a rare recording of one of the last surviving castrati and found it to be a weird and eerie sound; decidedly distinctive from the female soprano.* Castrati were active in the opera of the Baroque Period. Female roles would be taken by castrati and in an even stranger extension, male soprano parts would be written for male characters. In Handel's Opera *Julius Caeser*, for instance, the part of Caeser is written for castrato. The practice declined and died out by the Classical Period.

Countertenor
While it may seem related to the castrati tradition, the counter-tenor voice is not nearly so exotic or controversial, though it may strike some as peculiar who are not accustomed to it. A countertenor has a normal male voice but sings completely in the head voice or falsetto. The range is generally that of the normal alto. It is actually not uncommon to find this type of singing in rock music. The countertenor voice was favored and common in the Renaissance Period especially in England. It declined through the following centuries and has only reappeared actually in the last thirty years or so along with the renewed interest in Renaissance music. Modern performances of old English music would most likely include the countertenor voice, and now that excellent singers are available we sometimes hear countertenors taking parts written for the normal female alto.

What About Your Own Voice?

The human voice is obviously the most elemental, most natural vehicle for making music. All instruments are, to an extent, attempts at imitating the voice. The greatest compliment we pay a fine player is to say that he or she "sings" on the instrument. From a different point of view, many artist caliber instrumentalists insist that if they "had a voice," they would have no interest in playing an instrument. Darwin, in his *Descent of Man*, by way of making the point that speech developed from music, provides a clue as to why we find the singing voice so powerful in its ability to ellicit emotional response. He writes:

> "I conclude that musical notes and rhythms were first acquired by the male or female progenitors of mankind for the sake of charming the opposite sex. Thus musical tones became firmly associated with some of the strongest passions an animal is capable of feeling. . ."

If Darwin is right about this as the origin of music, then it would follow that the voice was certainly the first instrument and therefore most essentially and directly associated with these strong passions.

Because we communicate through speech, humans have acquired a highly-developed ability to distinguish very subtle differences and nuances of the voice. It does not take long before even a beginning listener will be able to identify the particular timbre of a favorite singer's voice. It is always fascinating and enlightening to listen and compare recordings of several different singers performing the same song or aria. It is interesting not only for the different styles and interpretations, but particularly for the colors, relative strengths and other hard-to-describe, but easy to hear differences that make every voice unique.

It is shocking how many people have no real idea of the characteristics or potential of their own voices. Unless you have studied voice or sung in a chorus with a highly analytical conductor who has thoroughly tested and evaluated your voice, and done this recently - that is, not as a child but as an adult - then you probably have no real idea about the characteristics of your own voice.

Unlike in swimming and tennis where individuals can reach a peak while still in their teens, the human voice does not mature until quite late. For the kind of singing demanded in art music, the voice typically matures and opens up in the mid-twenties and continues to darken and strengthen for years after that. It is a source of frustration that voice majors in college often do not have a real idea of the kind of voice they have to work with until five or so years after graduation. Yet if the voice does not have sufficient size and character, no amount of study or practice will produce a great singer.

On the other hand, it sometimes happens that a special voice develops in unlikely people. The author knows of a man in his late twenties, an auto mechanic, who discovered that , in the shower, he could sing with a voice like an opera singer. With encouragement from his wife he demonstrated for some musicians who confirmed that this was a tenor voice of rare size and quality and that something ought to be done with it. He has since sold his garage, studied for several years in New York, and has made a good start on a career as an operatic tenor, performing to great acclaim for audiences of thousands.

Sometimes you can get a good idea of a person's singing voice from listening to his or her speaking voice - but not always.   It is just as common to find that the speaking voice bears not the faintest resemblance to the singing voice.   The point is to make the reader aware that it is possible that they may have a hidden gift.   Make the effort to discover the potential in your own voice. Experimenting on your own may provide some idea, but a better way is to have a session with a good voice teacher, experienced in ferreting out the elusive singing voice.

A powerful voice does not guarantee fame and fortune as an opera star.   Musical ability, beyond sheer voice is required, along with training, commitment and the right personality.   But a good voice is a great and very personal gift; it should be, at the very least,   discovered and acknowledged.

When you have once encountered your voice and have some idea of its potential, you may be interested in pursuing a number of interesting possibilities: studying singing in a style of your choice, or singing for the pleasure it brings in one of the many choral groups to be found, of all types.   More on this in Chapter Eight.

CHAPTER EIGHT

Vocal Forms

Before considering the many forms taken by vocal music through the ages, a few words may be in order on the general subject of singing, particularly choral singing.

Participation in Choral Music

At the end of chapter seven the reader was encouraged to take steps to learn if he or she might be in possession of a voice of undiscovered potential. There is always the possibility that a voice of unusual greatness will be exposed. In this case the reader may feel a commitment to pursue training toward solo singing. You may discover, however, that your voice is more or less average, with some good points and some limitations. In any event it is your voice, the only one you will ever have, and in its own way a unique and special thing.

The author has spent many hours listening to student recitals at many levels of skill. They are not always edifying. One such obligation has been listening to end-of-semester juries for voice lessons. These sessions involving singing by students who have just begun the study of voice are, on the contrary, always interesting. The infinite variety of characteristics in the human voice is fascinating. Each has absolutely distinct qualities and despite imperfections and lack of technique, there is something highly satisfying about the display of voices.

It may be related to the satisfaction of people-watching in public places. We have a special fascination with the configuration of human faces, and we have a similar, special capacity to enjoy human voices. In his book, "The Dragons of Eden," Carl Sagan tells us that certain locations in the human brain are particularly well developed as compared to other organisms; the ability to recognize subtle differences in the human face is notable. Would investigation show that our capacity to distinguish subtleties in voice quality is equally strong?

Short of becoming a soloist, there are many excellent opportunities to sing, at any level of competence. To learn to play an instrument with the skill necessary to participate in even the most casual community group requires a substantial investment of time, energy and money. In addition it requires the ability to read music. But it is possible for singers to circumvent all of these hurdles.

There are professional groups where vocal training and the ability to read music are requirements. While these accomplishments certainly are welcome in any choral group, they are decidedly not required in a great many choruses to be found at schools, religious institutions, and amateur community groups.

The chorus has a huge and varied repertoire ranging from music of the medieval period through the most modern works, and from arrangements of folk songs and show tunes through challenging esoteric works of great complexity: the great masses, motets and oratorios. Joining one of these ensembles can afford great social activity along with, of course, real direct participation in an artistic venture. It is never too late in life to choose to be a personal participant in making music in the most natural way - with your own voice; among the very most satisfying and rewarding experiences life has to offer.

Choral singing is a phenomenon that extends back to the very beginnings of human history. We find it as an important activity in the most primitive societies. The natural inclination to join voices is so universally felt that it probably needs little explanation. One of the most unfortunate consequences of our TV addicted society may be that we do not have the kind of informal social opportunities to sing together that were more common in the past. Beyond social singing, participation in a chorus requires more time and effort, but offers an experience of greater artistic depth. Like the phenomenon of the orchestra, less colorful, but even more elemental in nature, the sound of the blending of many voices in a chorus is a phenomenon of transcendental beauty and wonderful expressive power.

Capable of the most ethereal, floating pianissimo (very soft) and earthshaking fortissimo (very loud) audible above the largest of orchestras, the chorus as a performing medium has attracted the great composers in their largest and most profound works. Of the works that are thought of as being the most monumental in the entire repertoire of music, most are works for chorus and orchestra: Bach's *Mass in B Minor*, and Beethoven's *Ninth Symphony*, foremost among them. (Most symphonies do not include chorus but Beethoven's *Ninth* does.)

There are some interesting differences in the make-up of choruses as opposed to orchestras. To be a part of a professional orchestra requires years of extensive professional training, great talent, diligent practice and considerable good fortune in the highly competitive audition process. Many extremely capable instrumentalists never succeed in securing a full time professional position.

There are a very few full time, professional choruses, maybe only three or four in the United States, and these are quite small, maybe twenty singers. They are engaged in specialized touring performances and recordings. These groups are made up of highly trained professional singers. Most of the famous and active large choruses that are an important part of the professional music scene are not professional groups, but choruses of colleges, churches or community groups. They appear on regular concert series with the finest orchestras, at major festivals and on professional recordings. The Mormon Tabernacle Choir, one of the finest and best known choruses in the world, is such a group.

In short, a decision to look into singing in a choral ensemble can, on one hand, offer great satisfaction on many levels, and participation in musical events of the highest caliber is not an unrealistic possibility for a talented but untrained latecomer.

Vocal Forms Through the Ages

In Chapter Five, we needed to go back only as far as the Baroque Period to find an established tradition of instrumental forms. But with vocal music we find more well-established forms beginning further back in history. Think for a moment about how you might characterize an attractive and interesting piece of music. You would probably include some of the following points:

- It should have interesting rhythmic characteristics.
- The melody should be easily recognizable with obvious high points.
- It should contain some contrast in dynamics (loud and soft).
- The form should be clear and interesting.
- It should hold the listener's attention.

The music that we will consider next will violate all of these principles.

Gregorian Chant

Gregorian chant is so named because in the time of Pope Gregory I (c. 540-604) codification was begun of the many chants in use in the Christian Church. These chants, thousands in number, were, and still are today, intoned by priests and monks in prayer services that occupied the many hours of their daily obligations. These chants of anonymous composition are, in effect, half prayer and half music. They are monophonic in texture, that is, one line of music with no counterpoint or harmony, and they follow a freely flowing rhythm, dictated by the Latin text, rather than any regular metric pattern.

There is an absence of large skips or characteristic melodic shapes; Gregorian Chants are not what you would describe as tuneful. The melodies flow freely with the text and have little feeling of tension and resolution; they are modal and therefore do not have a strong sense of tonality. Sung in unison by groups of medium ranged male voices, they include no particularly interesting tone colors.

If we were describing a popular song or a symphony here, we would have a remarkably poor piece on our hands, the worst criticism being that it would not hold anyone's attention. But when we consider that the purpose of Gregorian Chant was, on the contrary, not to call attention to itself, but rather to enhance group worship and to create an atmosphere for contemplation, these gently undulating melodies can be seen to have achieved a state of rare perfection.

Today you may encounter Gregorian Chants in several places. They are sometimes included as part of regular choral performance programs. They are also readily available on recordings. If you are in the mood for a kind of music that is soothing, relaxing and compatible with quiet contemplation you will find a recording of these chants highly satisfying.

The best way to experience Gregorian Chant, however, is to attend a church or cathedral where they are sung, as intended, as part of the daily worship service. You will find that the sound reverberating in the stone architecture, the visual elements and the genuine spiritual aura of the surroundings can all combine in a highly inspirational experience.

Joseph Kerman writes:

> Hearing traditional chant or later Medieval music today, one feels less like a "listener" in the modern sense than like a privileged eavesdropper, someone who has been allowed to attend a select occasion that is partly musical but mainly spiritual. The experience is an intimate and tranquil one, cool and (to some listeners) especially satisfying.

Folk Music

Our concern in this book is with art music. However the singing of a song is the most natural, human and universal of human activities. It is the wellspring from which other kinds of music flow and an ever present influence on art music through the centuries.

A folk song is defined as one which comes from the people, more often the poor or working classes. Although the song itself was most likely created by a specific individual, we do not know who the individual was. The song was sung to tell a story, inspired by some occasion, or created to serve a particular function (such as coordinating the raising of a ship's sail), and then either forgotten or passed on orally to other people and other generations, sometimes undergoing alterations and variations in the process. By nature, folk songs tend to be short and not highly complex. The form is usually simple, often dictated by the intended use of the song, and involves repetition. This is not to say that there is little of value in folk songs. On the contrary, they are of the greatest interest and particularly to musicians. Great composers have expressed high respect for folk music. Many have included folk tunes in their own larger works and several have been serious students and collectors of folk music; Haydn, Beethoven, Brahms and Bartok are among them.

Lute Song

When we think of modern folk music, probably the first image that comes to mind is someone singing, and at the same time, playing an accompaniment on the guitar. In fact, historically, folk music is, for the most part, sung without accompaniment. In England, however, particularly from 1590 to 1630, a form of art music developed which came to be known as the **lute song** or "ayre." Lute songs were composed for a singer accompanied by an instrument called the lute. Like a guitar but pear shaped, with a curved back and a more delicate sound, the lute was a popular instrument for solo works, small ensembles and accompanying. For the lute song, the instrument might be played by the singer while singing, or by another musician, a lutenist.

Lutenist

Lute songs were written by a group of highly accomplished composers, the greatest among them being John Dowland. While these works come from a time quite distant from our own, they remain highly enjoyable to the modern listener.   For one thing they are in English, specifically the idiom we are familiar with from Shakespeare; the poetry is always interesting and sometimes excellent.

Another very good reason to become acquainted with the lute song is that performances of these highly accessible works are becoming more common today, as our interest and understanding of Renaissance music has improved so greatly in recent years.

The Madrigal

At about the same time and place as the lute song (England, 1590-1620), a similar form appeared, but written for a group of from three to seven singers, usually unaccompanied. This form, imported from Italy, was the **Madrigal**. Using the same sort of texts, mainly about love, and some quite risque even by modern standards, the added parts made for a very pleasant mixing of homophony with polyphony. The English form of the madrigal is a logical starting place for listening. When a familiarity with these has been established, the Italian madrigal can be easily approached through many excellent examples.

Characteristic of the English madrigal are passages set to nonsense syllables of the "fa la la" variety. We also find the rise of what is called **word painting** where the composer tries to literally reflect the meaning of the words in the music: The words "Running up and down," would be set to a musical passage with rapidly ascending and descending scales etc. Madrigals are full of these devices and it makes careful listening very rewarding when they are discovered.

Part writing in the madrigal dictated that the singers have the ability to read music, a skill that was taken for granted, at the time, in anyone educated and well bred. Madrigals were intended for the enjoyment of the performers themselves rather than for large audiences, and were performed in small gatherings. If you are a singer, the best way to enjoy madrigals is to take part yourself. If you are not a singer you may still find these clever, charming and often beautiful works very entertaining to listen to. Recordings and live concerts have made madrigals accessible to all of us.

Two other vocal forms, the motet and the chanson, existed side by side for centuries. At times they were quite distinct and at other times their characteristics blended.

Motet

Taking its name from the French *mot*, which means "word," the motet was the name given to a great many vocal compositions from the 13th Century to the 18th Century. Gothic motets were written for three or four voices (some of these parts might be played by instruments) to a Latin text with one of the parts based on a stretched out Gregorian Chant, called a **cantus firmus**. The connection between the parts was looser than our ears are used to, both musically and textually: different voice parts would sometimes appear with melodies that sounded unrelated, with texts in different languages and on entirely different subjects sung simultaneously. A sacred text and an earthy love song, for example, might appear concurrently .

The form became more restrained and serious in the Renaissance period, as the motet was now more usually intended for worship. By this time all voices shared a common text. By the Baroque period, the term signified an unaccompanied, largely polyphonic vocal work of religious nature, but with a text in the vernacular.

Chanson

The chanson, taking it's name from the French word for "song," indicated a polyphonic setting for voices of a French love poem. The structure of the poetry served to shape the form of the musical work. The chanson developed parallel to the Motet and had a particular flowering around the 15th century in Burgundy. They were commonly written for three, and then later, four voices.

Compared to the motet they were generally more rhythmic, simpler, and more tuneful and folk-song like.

Cantata
The cantata was a name of Italian origin meaning "a piece to be sung," as opposed to the instrumental "sonata." The term applied to Baroque works both secular and sacred for a small group of vocal soloists, usually one or two, accompanied by either a small instrumental ensemble or a small orchestra.   Larger versions of the cantata added chorus to the performing group.   The cantata was similar to a scene from a Baroque opera, but not staged, with recitatives,   arias,   duets,   choruses   and   sometimes, instrumental movements.   A typical cantata lasts about twenty minutes.

Most notable are two hundred church cantatas by J.S. Bach, comprising several cycles of works for each of the weeks of the church calendar.

Mass And Requiem
For 800 years composers have set to music the Mass, the central worship service of the Christian Church.   The tradition carries on today in the Catholic service.   Through the centuries the music of the Mass has changed character with the styles of the times while some elements remain constant.   The sections of the regular version of the Mass, called the Ordinary, are: *Kyrie, Gloria, Credo, Sanctus and Agnus Dei.*   These constitute the individual movements of the musical setting.

The usual setting of the mass is for chorus and orchestra, with parts for vocal soloists often included. Fragments of Gregorian Chant traditionally serve as a unifying factor used as a basis for sections throughout the Mass.

The Requiem, a Mass for the dead, omits the _Credo_ and _Gloria_ and adds a _Dies Irae_ section depicting the day of judgement. By nature, the Mass and Requiem are serious and important works. As you might imagine, the centuries, combined with various great minds and spirits, have given us through these awe inspiring forms some of the most sublime and moving of all human creations.

Oratorio

The oratorio is a form that evolved in the later years of the Baroque period. It is very much like Baroque opera except that it is not staged, but presented in what we call "concert form" - no sets, costumes or acting. Singers do, however, represent characters, and, aside from the greater importance of the chorus, many musical details are indistinguishable from opera. Forces called for are solo voices, chorus and orchestra. The text is usually of a religious or serious nature. Handel's _Messiah_ is a famous example. The **Passion** is a particular kind of oratorio, specifically dealing with the Christian story of the last days of Christ.

Art Song

The song is such an elemental and natural form that it is present throughout history either as folk song or written by composers of art music. From time to time, however, the song form takes on special significance. We have considered one of these times in the above section on the lute song.

Another time of heightened activity in the composition of songs was the Romantic period, particularly starting with the works of Franz Schubert. Schubert brought a special genius to the writing of songs, composing more than 600 in his tragically short life of 31 years. We refer to these songs and the songs of other German composers after Schubert as *lieder*, the German word for songs, the singular form being *lied*.

As perfected by Schubert, the *lied* in the nineteenth century was a short work for solo voice, usually not requiring the great virtuosity demanded of opera singing. The songs were settings of verse by contemporary German poets, many of them, like Goethe and Heine, the leading poets of the day. This fusion of music and poetry was of great significance in the success of the form. The song was accompanied by the piano, often in a way that gave the instrument an important role in contributing to the mood of the work.

Depending on the poetry involved, the song would take one of several forms. **Strophic form** used repetition of the musical material to changing verses of the poem. **Through-composed** songs used less repetition and the form followed the structure of the poem freely from beginning to end.

Composers would sometimes create a set of lieder intended to be performed together; the effect would be to establish a plot or story of sorts, tying the songs together to make a larger composite form called a **song cycle.**

Through Schubert's influence, the art song has been an important concern of many fine composers right up to the present, leaving us with a varied array of these small but wonderful and uniquely engaging works.

CHAPTER NINE

Styles

Our look at styles will be limited, and specific discussion of historical events and influences purposely kept to a minimum. This can be somewhat frustrating to the intellectually curious student, or those inclined toward scholarly inquiry. Once you have experienced the music itself, the study of music history might begin in earnest. Many excellent music history books are available as are courses that are actually dedicated to and called "Music History." This subject has much of great value and interest to offer and will only increase the understanding and enjoyment that attends the actual experience of listening.

One might take the attitude that music is to listen to, not to read or study about. If we hear music and we do not like it, even after repeated listenings, well then, reading or studying about it will not cause it to sound any better. On the other hand we have considered that focusing attention, rather than mindless listening, is more likely to reveal the less obvious virtues of a work and certainly makes the process of coming to know it faster.

There is also a curious inclination shared by many members of the human species: We like to know about the things we love, music included. Knowing what it is called and learning about origins and characteristics helps us to think about music. We also need to know some of these things in order to communicate about the music that we are trying to understand; to talk about it and to read about it.

The ability to listen to a musical work and identify it by sound is a case in point. It is a mark of erudition for an individual to hear a few moments of music and be able to say, "Hmm... sounds like late Classical; probably one of the Beethoven Piano Concertos." This ability to broadly classify works according to style period is basic and worth acquiring. It is an enjoyable skill to have. You will impress yourself with your cultural sophistication. Some of this ability is naturally earned through listening experience. Styles just begin to sound familiar. You will know that a work is from the Classical period, for instance, without specifically knowing why. But a basic familiarity with the traditional style periods can strengthen and quicken the process.

Style Periods

Music In The Ancient World

It is well documented that music has existed since man has been living in any kind of societal structure.

Archaeological digs unearth crude instruments of music as evidence. The bible provides multiple reference to the important place of music, both in ceremony and in everyday life. Ancient Greek civilization held music as a fundamental requirement of education, as different modes of music were believed to cause strong, profound and direct changes in the human psyche. Unfortunately, however, all of this came and went before a viable system of notation had been established. The result is that we can only guess what this music actually sounded like.

Medieval 400-1450

It was not until approximately 1100 that a system of notation developed sufficiently so that we are today able to have an accurate idea of how the music of the time was intended to sound. At around 1100, the decision was made to preserve in writing the body of Gregorian Chant which had been composed and codified over the previous several hundred years. Gregorian Chant, of course, with its monophonic texture and highly distinctive sound is easily identifiable.

Homophonic music is so natural to us today that it is hard to imagine that in the relatively recent era of one thousand years ago, the idea of more than one note at a time was new. Polyphony began somewhat haphazardly, almost experimentally, with two melodies happening at the same time. At first the melodies were not highly related; they were new at this. The results were often interesting and eventually led to great things, but to our ears, the music can sound poorly organized. It is not unusual for the parts to clash, resulting in jarring dissonances.

The orchestra had not been established yet. Medieval music is for small groups of voices or mixed voices and instruments.   The texture is either monophonic or polyphonic, with little imitation between the parts and a lack of underlying harmony. The tonality is modal and rhythm tends to be limited to repetitions of the same patterns. It is not unusual to find different sets of words to the different parts, sometimes in different languages, and, possibly, both sacred and secular texts; all in the same piece. Medieval works often use an elongated section of Gregorian Chant as an underlying, unifying element (called *cantus firmus.*)

You will not encounter a great deal of the music of the Middle Ages in our everyday musical life. Performances can be found, but by groups that specialize in early music, and in special historical and scholarly presentations. If you find an opportunity to attend one of these you will probably notice that the music sounds strange, crude and half-formed. The glimpse that it affords us of the evolutionary process is interesting in its own right, but equally important is the fact that, despite its primitive construction, it often has a strange, archaic fascination for us, an appeal familiar to us from the world of primitive art; and much of it is put together with real genius.

Renaissance 1450-1600
Generally, music of the Renaissance has a more refined sound than that of the Middle Ages. The texture is still essentially polyphonic, but now we find more imitation of melodic material back and forth between the different voices. Compared to the previous period, Renaissance music has a somewhat fuller, more integrated harmonic sound. The older tendency to repeat the same rhythmic figures throughout a piece has given way to much greater variation in patterns. Direct expression of emotion through the music is handled somewhat dispassionately and with re-

serve. If it is very big, very long, and very loud, it is probably not music of the Renaissance Period.

Instruments were becoming somewhat more standardized, often being built in sets or families of different sizes. Composers still treated them, however, without a great deal of concern for the instruments' individual characters. Often an instrument was used to substitute for a voice, and writing for instruments tended to be very much the same as vocal writing. Instrumental virtuosity was not yet an important factor, although music for the lute was an exception, and some highly idiomatic music was produced for this instrument.

The feeling of tonality in Renaissance music was stronger and more evident than in the Middle Ages. Although major and minor tonalities became more common, the modes, with their gentler sense of tonality, still prevailed.

Baroque 1600-1750

An important development in the music of the Baroque period was the rise of dramatic expression. Composers wrote in a way that was more subjective and emotionally direct, with larger, deeper feelings more prominently displayed. Works tended to be longer than in the Renaissance, often on a larger scale and often more spectacular. Baroque music frequently conveys a sense of grandeur. More and greater contrasts are noticeable.

Baroque harmony developed a stronger and more organized sense of progression. Although polyphony is still the prevailing texture, this is the era that saw homophony become much more well established. It was not unusual to have homophonic and polyphonic textures in contrasting sections of the same piece. The use of the basso continuo was almost universal in the Baroque, and is related to the tendency of interest to gravitate to the top and bottom parts, especially in homophonic textures. The bass line became second in importance only to the melody.

This is the period in which the modes gave way to major and minor scales. Since most music written since then has maintained the use of the major-minor system, we find that, harmonically, Baroque music sounds less strange and archaic than that of the preceding periods.

A new rhythmic vitality entered Baroque music. Slow movements could convey an ongoing sense of flow. Fast movements were inhabited by an energetic, spirited feeling of momentum, often with great bounce and drive.

For the first time, instrumental parts became distinctly different from vocal parts. The perfection of the violin family and improvements in the development of other instruments gave rise to a new virtuosity which was reflected in written instrumental music parts.

Contrasts in dynamics, for instance, were expected of performers, though not yet always indicated in the written scores.   Rather than calling for gradual increases and decreases in dynamics, composers thought in terms of adding or subtracting forces, causing clearly defined, contrasting levels of dynamics: Ranks of pipes on the organ, sets of strings on the harpsichord, or groups of instruments in the orchestra - the concerto grosso uses this idea as an important central focus. This is called **terraced dynamics**, and is one of the clear earmarks of the Baroque Period.

Although organ music was composed in other periods as well, this instrument reached its greatest prominence in the Baroque era; particularly with the many masterful works of J.S. Bach. If you hear an organ, chances are good that the music is from the Baroque Period. This is even more true of the harpsichord. It has been called for by twentieth century composers, but very rarely, and then usually to evoke an antiquated atmosphere. (The harpsichord was entirely absent from the Romantic Period, having been replaced by the piano early in the Classical Period.) Extremely high and brilliant trumpet parts are another good instrumental clue that you are listening to Baroque music.

Classical 1750-1825

The pendulum swings back, from the pathos of the Baroque Period to ethos in the Classical. The overall atmosphere of Classical music is one of refinement, elegance and grace. Gone are the excesses of outward emotion found in the Baroque. Rather, it is more accurate to recognize that composers still found ways to make their works expressive, but now the emotion was veiled; hidden beneath a carefully ordered and controlled exterior.

Although some counterpoint was still in use, homophony was the order of the day. Dissonance was at a minimum, appearing only as an occasional twinge. Musical phrases were clear and well defined as were the larger sectional structures. This is the era when Sonata-allegro form evolved and exerted its greatest influence.

Gradual changes in dynamics, the crescendo and diminuendo, entered the musical vocabulary0 and dynamics were generally given more attention, but, as in all aspects of classicism, with restraint, always and in everything.

Romantic 1825-1900

With the Romantic period the pendulum of expression returns to the pathos side. The tendency to exaggerate was evident in many areas. Pieces grew to be both very long and very short. Composers called for fortissimos and pianissimos (very loud and very soft.) The orchestra expanded, and by the end of the era had more than doubled in size. Orchestral color and the art of orchestration gained greatly in importance. The instruments themselves evolved to play louder and higher. In the opera house the human voice was pushed beyond the limits of past ages, reaching new heights of power and range.

Homophony continued to dominate the harmonic language, but it was a homophony that now included greater levels of dissonance and an ever expanding vocabulary of chords.

Whereas Classical music had gone in the direction of an international blending of styles, the Romantic trend was to rediscover national characteristics and to make extensive use of these characteristics in composition.

Twentieth Century 1900-?

Until this century there were certainly differences in style from one region to another, and from one composer to another, but they were relatively small differences. Unique though they were, all composers shared a great many characteristics, common characteristics that defined the style period to which they belonged. This situation came to a sudden halt with the advent of the twentieth century.

If there is a common characteristic of modern music it is probably to display no common characteristic. The need to do something new was a very powerful force. Composers seemed to feel that it was important to have their own unique style, and beyond that to demonstrate that this style was changing with each new piece.

As a result, it is most difficult to compile a list of characteristics for modern music. Whatever can be said about one piece, another example will demonstrate a diametrically opposed concept. Could it be that the best way to identify a composition from the twentieth century is by a process of elimination; if it does not sound like it belongs in one of the other periods, then it might be modern? Right from the beginning, this century has given us opposites: Very simple and very complex, serious and irreverent, highly controlled and completely uncontrolled (serial and aleatory).

In general, compared to music of past centuries, there is more dissonance; harmonies and rhythms have become more complex, meters and tonality have become more obscure, counterpoint is the prevalent texture and sonorities are lighter.

Never before has there existed the kind of chasm that we have had in this century between popular music and art music. The philosophical implications of this situation are far reaching.

Following is a list of some influential movements and names of composers who may have been particularly associated with them:

Primitivism: Stark, angular rhythms and melodic lines. Stravinsky.

Dodecaphony: Also known as twelve-tone composition. Developed by Arnold Schoenberg, a serial system for composing that treats all twelve tones equally, usually resulting in atonality. Many composers used this system either sometimes or always.

Serialism: Composition using a pre-determined series of notes in recurring order.   Specific rules and procedures apply.

Neobaroque: Highly influenced by, and reminiscent of, Baroque music. Stravinsky, Hindemith.

Neoclassicism: Highly influenced by, and reminiscent of, Classical music.

Neoromanticism: Highly influenced by, and reminiscent of, Romantic music. Appeared in the last part of the century, later than post-romanticism.

Dadaism: Irreverent ridiculing of art music conventions sometimes   resulting   in   shocking   or   silly compositions. Satie.

Aleatory: Otherwise known as chance music.   The composer allows random events to determine some or all of the elements of the composition.   John Cage.

Electronic: Music using tone generators and synthesizers both for composition and performance.

Post-Romantic: Music by composers who continued to write in an essentially Romantic style with some more modern techniques. Richard Strauss, Rachmaninoff.

Atonality: Music that does not convey a feeling of tonality or key center.

CHAPTER TEN

Composers

Studying the lives of composers has been a traditional component of learning about music, just as it has been considered worthwhile to have some idea about the lives of historically significant statesmen, inventors, scientists, conquerors, etc. The explanation of why we do this is probably quite involved; there is no simple and obvious reason for acquiring these facts. Whether Napoleon was short or tall had no bearing on the effects his actions had on the history of world events. Or did it? There are those who believe that it may well have had a crucial effect, and that the most important things we can learn are just those things that directly have to do with people.

Even though we may occasionally wonder about the value of delving into the lives, values and relationships of the creators of music, and even though it is true that nothing we learn about them will change a note of the music they have left us, we may still recognize that, in the largest sense, this inquiry is not only valid, but appropriate and natural.

For the arts, these ideas hold doubly true.   It is generally accepted that on the deepest level, the arts have meaning for us because they are analogous to life.   What more appropriate place to look for the significance of life in general than in the specific, actual life that gave rise to the music?

Philosophy aside, lives of the great composers are interesting.   They have inspired many excellent biographical studies over the years and there is often plentiful material, especially with the Romantic composers, sufficient to provide a full and detailed picture.   It seems that most composers, almost regardless of the ultimate degree of success they might have achieved, lived and worked in centers of cultural and political import.   Along with this, of course, the circles they were active in often included individuals of historical interest: Mozart met Marie Antoinette, Beethoven knew Goethe, Mendelssohn was a frequent visitor to, and friendly with Queen Victoria, Bach had lively discussions with Frederick the Great.

Often the lives of composers are, in and of themselves, of great interest.   Take, for example, the success of the play and subsequent film, *Amadeus*, based on the life and death of Mozart.   The story of Robert Schumann, his love for Clara, their struggle to marry against her father's will, Robert's tragic death and the ensuing relationship of Brahms and Clara is a classic epic worthy of the most tumultuous romantic literature of the age.

But what makes getting to know a composer very special is the connection with the music itself.   This adds a whole new dimension. Listening to music while or after learning about a composer's life invests both experiences with intensified meaning. In the music, we find the ideas and emotions made manifest. We learn what the composer was experiencing and what he or she said or wrote (in words) about it, and then we turn to the music, where we hear these things transformed into the language of tones, the essential nature of which is to miraculously convey the actuality, the reality, of the emotion to the listener.

If you doubt this, read Beethoven's letter known as the Heiligenstadt Testament, in which the composer reveals that seriously increasing deafness (he was thirty two at the time) had driven him to the brink of suicide. But he tells us also of overcoming his despair:

> "I am resolved to rise superior to every obstacle. With whom need I be afraid of measuring my strength? I will take Fate by the throat. It shall not overcome me. Oh how beautiful it is to be alive - Would that I could live a thousand times!"

Listen to the last few minutes of the Egmont Overture and you will hear, and you will feel, the greatness of Beethoven's soul, the power of his will to survive and the triumph of the human spirit over adversity.

The following are brief introductory sketches of some of the most celebrated of composers. The decision as to which to include and, especially, which to exclude is troublesome and arguments could be made in favor of a number of excellent musicians who are not included. The fifteen presented here, however, are all worthy of being part of any list of first rank composers.

Johann Sebastian Bach 1685-1750

When the question of the greatest composer of all time comes up, Bach is usually the first mentioned.   His compositions were not outwardly innovative and he was not involved in creating new forms and styles, but what he did, all within the bounds of the conventional mature Baroque style, he accomplished with awesome skill.   Bach's ability to control the technical aspects of music has never been equalled.   Even more phenomenal, and the real source of this composer's greatness, was his ability to make his unsurpassed technical powers serve expressive ends.   No matter how complex the writing became, he was able to convey the full range of human feelings, powerfully and deeply, transcending time and place.   His compositions, for this reason, are a monument to the universal human spirit, and at the same time, for those who seek it, a treasure of great personal satisfaction.

He was born in Germany and never travelled out of the country. Orphaned at the age of ten, he went to live with an older brother, also a musician. He was a musician in a family of musicians; his grandfathers, father, brothers and sons were all professional music makers. The women in the family were also musicians, but in keeping with conventions of the times, did not have opportunities for accomplishment outside the home.

Bach did not gain widespread recognition during his lifetime, but worked at a series of moderately responsible posts as a court composer and particularly as a church musician, most notably as cantor, organist and choirmaster of St. Thomas Church in Leipzig, Germany. He was know as an organist of great skill and probably enjoyed more of a reputation for his playing than for his composing. Unlike the modern tendency of musicians to specialize in either performing, conducting, or composing, Baroque musicians were expected to be more well rounded, complete musicians, able to play, teach and direct performances and of course, to compose. Even for the time, however, Bach was unusually gifted and would confound listeners, skilled and unskilled alike, with incredible displays of on-the-spot improvisation, for which he had an uncanny ability.

A dedicated husband and father, he lost his first wife to illness and then remarried.   All told he had twenty children, though, typical of the period, they did not all survive infancy. Aside from some arguments with church and town officials - at one point he spent a month in jail because he insisted on resigning his post to take another job - his life was not particularly eventful. He did his job, raised his family and was not afforded any unusual recognition beyond the admiration of some astute musicians who realized that something extraordinary was being produced.   Even his sons, four of whom became the leading composers of the next generation, came to consider their father's music old-fashioned, although in later years they were also proud to acknowledge the old man's unsurpassed skill and musicianship.

Blind in his last years, he continued to compose, dictating to one of his daughters.   That we mark the end of the Baroque period with his death in 1750 is more than a coincidence; he had brought the style to perfection, and, in the process, created a body of immortal music.

Bach composed in all Baroque forms with the exception of opera.   His output was staggering, both for its volume and for its quality.   His compositions for the organ constitute the foundation of the literature for the instrument.   He became absolute master of every form he attempted.

Bela Bartok 1881-1945

Bartok chose to follow his own convictions rather than subscribe to the many established currents, movements and "isms" in twentieth century composition.   The style that resulted, has proven to be among the most personal and successful of the century.

Though he is considered to be the great representative and spokesman for Hungarian music, he was actually born in the Torontal district which is now part of Rumania, an indication of the chaotic shifting of national borders in this region in the twentieth century. A prodigy on the piano, he began performing in public at the age of eleven. As a young man Bartok became fascinated with the folk and peasant music of his native land and embarked on a major project to collect and preserve what he felt were imminently disappearing examples of indigenous Hungarian music. He travelled widely in Hungary, recording, cataloguing and codifying, becoming, with his friend and fellow musician, Zoltan Kodaly, a world authority on the folk music of Hungary.

His own direction as a musician shifted to include composition in addition to his career as piano virtuoso. His interest in folk music, however, directly influenced his composing. He believed that the true course for a Hungarian composer was to:

> "assimilate the idiom of peasant music so completely that he is able to forget all about it and use it as his mother tongue."

By all measures he appears to have succeeded in his theoretical plan, producing a kind of music substantially Hungarian in sound, but without using actual folk material. His writing shares some characteristics with the music of other contemporary composers in that it contains considerable dissonance and uses highly complex rhythmic patterns, often with a savage ferocity. On first hearing, this music strikes many as exotic, but also somewhat harsh and severe. Familiarity, however, usually reveals logic, deep feeling and, for many listeners, highly exciting, attractive and moving music.

As an individual with great national pride, he was appalled at the impending takeover of his homeland by

Hitler's Nazis and he determined to leave the country.   At the age of fifty eight he came to the United States.

Although never celebrated or highly famous during his lifetime, he was respected in musical circles as a fine pianist and a true nationalist composer.   He earned a modest living between composing and his work at Columbia University, where he held a position allowing him to continue researching Hungarian folk music.

It was only after his death in New York at the age of 64 that he became widely acknowledged as a composer of highly individual style and one who had managed to successfully reconcile many of the problems of twentieth century art music.

The musical language he created out of peasant music roots was seen to be, at the same time, a logical, natural extension of the heritage of nineteenth century art music, and a true and viable twentieth century utterance. In the process, he left us music of unusual power, uncompromising integrity, and great expressiveness.

Ludwig Van Beethoven 1770-1827

Only one composer can be the greatest of all time, and we have already nominated Bach for that distinction. If not for Bach, Beethoven would surely qualify and, in all fairness, there are many that would reverse the order. The question is actually of limited validity since greatness is so subjective a commodity, but, at the risk of being overly philosophical, it can be said with confidence that when it comes to *expressing* greatness in music, Beethoven has no peer.

He was born in a small town in Germany to a family of modest means.   Both his father and grandfather were professional musicians but of no great distinction.   His father, having heard of the boy genius Mozart, and believing reports, largely unfounded, of the great wealth he had won in his world travels, began a program of training for young Ludwig with the intention of developing a second "wunderkind."   But Ludwig, though talented, was not the kind of genius Mozart had been, and even more to the point, his father was not the equal of Mozart's in providing guidance, encouragement and instruction.   The outcome was unhappy for the young musician, who suffered abuse from his bad tempered, frequently drunken father.

Though he did not become a prodigy, he did develop into a skilled musician.   His early compositions showed distinctive character and he became a pianist of astounding technical and expressive power.   He had a rare talent for improvisation   and   a   reputation   for   spellbinding performances.   In these, he was reported to engage audiences in trancelike states of absorption, so great was his power to communicate and express strong emotion through music.

Though he was largely self educated, emotional by nature, somewhat overbearing and moody, he was accepted in high and aristocratic social circles on the merit of his great talent and strong, outgoing personality.   He moved to Vienna as a young man where he studied composition with Joseph Haydn and seemed on the verge of a successful career as pianist and composer.   It was at this time that his hearing began to suffer the deterioration that would eventually lead to deafness.

Struggling against despair, he overcame his tragic loss of hearing and, since his career as a pianist was destroyed, he turned solely to composition. For a composer of Beethoven's ability, creating music is largely an internal process. Although he no doubt suffered greatly from his deafness, it did not prevent him from composing, though he was never to hear his greatest compositions.

He was the first major composer to earn a living, essentially, in the free market, without the patronage of a court or church. Mozart, several years earlier, had attempted this but without real success. Beethoven, with his strong personality and a belief in the value of the individual, insisted on being treated with respect, refusing to bow to the aristocracy, both literally and figuratively.

He lived alone, often in poor health, creating the masterpieces that would change the direction of music from the style of the Classical age to that of the Romantic. He died a famous man, in Vienna; appropriately, during a thunderstorm. Even today, almost two hundred years later, passages of his works strike us as arresting and unconventional.

Leonard Bernstein pointed out that Beethoven had the great ability to compose music that was, at the same time, unexpected and yet entirely right sounding; surprising and yet inevitable. In his music, to a great extent, we recognize the trials and the triumphs of human existence, sorrows and ecstacies. No other composer can convey, like Beethoven, the sense of surmounting and triumphing over life's adversities. It may be due to his struggle with deafness, and probably is, at least in part, but we can hear these things even in some of his earliest works; a product of a unique creative gift, coupled with an innately, stormy and emotional nature.

Johannes Brahms 1833-1897

Probably the most highly respected composer of the late Romantic period, Brahms was born just after Beethoven's death and lived into the last years of the century. His complex personality and connection with important issues and individuals have made his life the subject of fascinating biographical studies.

He was born in Hamburg, Germany, the son of a not very successful musician who played the string bass. Brahms, by the age of thirteen, was a gifted pianist. Instead of a concert hall debut, however, his first engagements were in Hamburg's waterfront bars where he played dance music for an audience of prostitutes and their patrons.   At twenty he had begun composing and had established the beginnings of a reputation as a concert pianist. He was heard by the highly influential composer Robert Schumann, who hailed the talents of the younger man in a famous magazine article.   Typical of his character, Brahms was very grateful, but at the same time apprehensive about fulfilling the expectations that Schumann's praise would inevitably raise.

Schumann's wife was the celebrated pianist Clara Schumann. A great friendship developed between young Brahms and the Schumanns. Robert's worsening mental condition resulted in an attempt to drown himself, followed by his commitment to a mental institution. Brahms helped greatly to pull Clara and her six children through the ordeal. Clara was fourteen years older than Brahms, but when her husband died soon thereafter they acknowledged a mutual love for one another. They did not marry, however, but remained very close in a relationship that has given rise to numerous biographical studies over the years.

In personality he was outwardly shy, and gave a gruff impression, but he was found to be thoughtful, sensitive and altogether highly likeable by those that came to know him.

Moving to Vienna, he pursued a life of composing and occasionally playing or conducting. Always careful and concerned with his reputation, he made a point of destroying much of his own music if he did not feel it met the highest standards. He waited for years - until the age of forty-three - to complete his first symphony. He strongly felt the responsibility of carrying on the tradition of the great composers who had come before him and said of Beethoven, "You have no idea how the likes of us feel when we hear the footsteps of a giant like him behind us."

He had a keen interest in older music and studied and collected much. His own music reflected this, being Romantic in essential style, but embodying many characteristics and ideals of the Classical age; especially a concern for the integrity of form. He composed brilliantly in all of the then current forms, with the exception of opera.

A controversy arose pitting the adherents of the music of Richard Wagner against those who saw Brahms as the true champion. Although Wagner joined in the debate personally, Brahms remained aloof, preferring to ignore it.

He was deeply saddened by the death of his friend Clara, in 1896, and died himself the following year, rightly mourned as the great master he had proven himself to be.

Frederic Chopin 1810-1849
Chopin is a rarity among great composers; he limited his composition exclusively to works for the piano, creating a unique and effective style of great elegance, and music greatly loved by unending generations, both of pianists and listeners.

He was born in Warsaw, Poland and became a highly acclaimed pianist while still in his teens. It was when he was 21 years old and traveling in Europe on a concert tour that Russia invaded Poland. Since it was not possible for him to return home, Chopin moved to Paris. A longing for his homeland and sadness at the fate of his countrymen affected him deeply.

Once settled in Paris, however, he established a reputation as one of the foremost pianists of the day, though his small, delicate physical condition did not lend itself to the very powerful, bombastic aspects of virtuoso performance. He became known for a new style of pianism: elegant, eloquent, poetic and atmospheric.

Basically shy, he avoided performing before large concert hall audiences, preferring instead to play for smaller, more intimate gatherings in the salons of Paris.

His writing was perfectly suited to the piano, an instrument that he knew so well.   The spirit, forms, melodies and characteristic rhythms of his native Poland were reflected in many of his compositions. He excelled in the creation of highly evocative, very short, character pieces.

He became involved in a love affair with Madame Aurore Dudevant, the writer better known by her pen name, George Sand. She was an early feminist who often dressed in men's clothing and smoked a cigar.   Their relationship lasted for nine years during which she cared for Chopin in his usually frail health and inspired many of his greatest compositions.

When their relationship ended Chopin ceased composing, his health deteriorated, and he died of tuberculosis at the age of thirty-nine.

Claude Debussy 1862-1918

Debussy occupies a unique place in the history of music.   He was one of the last composers of Romantic Music, and at the same time one of the first to write in a style that clearly influenced the direction of composition throughout the twentieth century.   From still another perspective he is the creator and chief proponent of a unique and individual style: Impressionism.

Debussy was born in a small town not far from Paris and, from the age of ten until he was twenty-two, attended the famous Paris Conservatory.   During this time he established a reputation as a highly talented pianist, and a composer of considerable promise, though he impressed his professors with an inclination toward the unconventional and a rebelliousness in the matter of conforming to rules of composition.   As a result of winning the coveted Prix de Rome, at the age of twenty two, he was invited to spend three years studying in Italy.   He chose to return to Paris in the third year.

This, of course, was the Paris of the Impressionist painters, and listening to the music of Debussy invariably calls to mind the dreamy, nebulous, beautiful but obscure scenes of Renoir and Monet. In fact, he created a style, influenced by the time, the place, and the events around him, but nevertheless entirely original: **Impressionism.** It is significant that one of his best known works is *Claire de Lune,* - *Moonlight.*

Debussy was strongly influenced by sounds brought to Paris from the Far East. Strange, oriental sounding scales and an exotic, Asian feeling found their way into much of what he wrote.   He was, by his own estimation, slow to fully mature as a composer, but by the time he reached his mid-thirties, he had completed a number of acknowledged masterworks, including his famous, *Prélude a "L'Apres-midi d'un Faune" (Prelude to "The Afternoon of a Faun.")*

His personal life was complicated by a series of problematic love affairs and two marriages.   Twice his affairs ended in tragedy when, upon Debussy's leaving one lover for another, the deserted women shot themselves. Extravagant living on the part of both himself and his wives caused serious and ongoing financial problems throughout his life.

Events leading up to World War I influenced a renewed sense of patriotism in this greatest of the French composers. He died of cancer at the age of 56.

George Frideric Handel 1685-1759

Along with Bach, who was born in the same year, Handel brought the Baroque period to culmination. He wrote music for all the current Baroque media, but made a particular success of a form that he perfected: the oratorio.

Although he spent the majority of his creative life in England, he was born in Halle, Germany. He was an avid student of music, though his father wanted him to study law, and became a skilled player of violin and particularly harpsichord and organ. Throughout most of his career he could count on drawing an enthusiastic audience to hear him perform his own keyboard works.

Italian opera was being performed all over Europe. At the age of 21, Handel composed one himself, soon after being engaged as an orchestra player at the Hamburg Opera. When it was accepted and produced, Handel was encouraged to travel to Italy where he spent three years studying, composing, and impressing the musical world with his considerable talent.

He returned to Germany where he was employed by the Elector George Ludwig of Hanover. He visited England to attend the performance of one of his operas and realized the potential there for artistic and financial success; so, soon after he returned to Hanover in 1712 he requested a short leave of absence to return to London. The short leave lasted for the rest of his life.

He wrote and produced, in all, thirty-nine Italian operas, becoming famous and celebrated in the process. A source of concern for him, no doubt, was that his former employer, George of Hanover, to whose service Handel had never returned, now became George I, King of England; but Handel regained his favor. The famous *Water Music* was composed by Handel to be performed on a barge accompanying a royal boat party.

He was a man of large size and outgoing personality. His heavy German accent and famous temper, which showed frequently, and especially when he worked with *Prima Donnas* in the opera house, made him a well known figure in gossipy London society. But social and political changes conspired to make Italian opera suddenly unfashionable, causing Handel, who was the owner of the entire operation as well as composer, to lose a fortune. He suffered two nervous breakdowns, but finally found new success in shifting his efforts to the English language oratorio. His works in this form, including the widely loved *Messiah*, have been frequently performed ever since.

Like Bach, he lost his sight in his last years. He died at the age of 74 and is buried in Westminster Abbey.

Joseph Haydn   1732-1809

Born in the same year as George Washington, Haydn is one of only two in the first rank of composers in the Classical period (assuming that we consider Schubert and Beethoven as transitional or early Romantic composers). The other is Mozart.   If Mozart and Haydn had not achieved so incomparably high a level of excellence, we might be concerned with the music of a great many other highly able composers of the time, but, as it happens, Mozart and Haydn clearly tower above their contemporaries.

He was born in a small town in Austria, the son of a wheelmaker.   His musical ability was noted and he was sent, at eight years of age, to be a choirboy in Vienna.

When his voice changed he was dismissed and found himself on the streets of Vienna. He gave lessons, played in street bands, taught himself about the instruments and began to compose, gradually gaining recognition.

When he was twenty-nine he was engaged by the Esterhazy family, wealthy Hungarian noblemen. This was a major turning point and he was to retain this appointment for the remainder of his life. For the next thirty years, in fact, he produced music almost exclusively for the Esterhazy Court. The next generation of composers, Mozart and Beethoven in particular, were to rebel against the near enslavement of the patronage system in which a composer was treated as a servant, but Haydn thrived on it. He was delighted to have an orchestra to write for, and though the demands were heavy he met them eagerly, producing a staggering volume of music including over one hundred symphonies. Especially in the symphonies, but also in the string quartets, he is credited as the principal architect of both form and style.

He is known to have had an unhappy marriage. Recent biographies indicate that he was involved in an affair with a singer at the Esterhazy court which caused considerable stress in the life of this otherwise well adjusted composer and resulted in music of unusually unsettled and emotional character in his middle years.

He came to know and greatly respect Mozart (who was younger by 24 years) and they learned greatly from one another. A particular trademark of Haydn is a musical sense of humor. Haydn knows what we are expecting and greatly enjoys denying, or at least delaying, these expectations. The listener is often fooled, but always with great wit and masterful good humor.

He was released from almost all of his obligations with the Esterhazys in his late years and found himself not only free but famous. He was invited twice to England where he was greeted with great acclaim. He died at the age of 77.

Wolfgang Amadeus Mozart 1756-1791

One of the greatest natural geniuses that ever lived, Mozart began composing at the age of 5. His father, Leopold Mozart, was a prominent court musician in the Austrian town of Salzburg, and carefully cultivated the education and career of his young genius. As a young boy, little Mozart toured the great courts of Europe, amazing all with his ability to play the violin and piano, to improvise and to compose. Wherever he went, he earned fame, some gold trinkets as gifts from the nobility, and absorbed languages, culture and a knowledge of diverse styles of music. It was widely supposed that he must have earned great wealth along with his fame, but it was not true.

As a young man he was not content with life in Salzburg and, against his father's objections, made himself uncooperative and disobedient enough that he was released from what would no doubt have been a comfortable position in the employ of the Archbishop of Salzburg.

He moved to Vienna, the center of European cultural life where he made a living by doing some performing, some teaching and writing music on commission. He also composed several operas which were performed. Again acting against his fathers advice, he married. Though he was well known and highly respected, especially by the few musicians distinguished enough to recognize the phenomenal perfection of his work, his income did not keep up with the family's expenses and he fell into debt.

The most prodigiously gifted of composers, Mozart, from childhood, had the ability to play or write out a musical work after hearing it only once. Where other composers toiled and struggled to compose, Mozart would essentially complete a work in his mind and then commit it to paper in one effortless flow, as though copying.

The rest of the story is short and sad: He fell ill and died shortly after the presentation of his last opera, *The Magic Flute*, leaving his wife, Constanza, two young sons, an unfinished *Requiem Mass* and a legacy of hundreds of radiant masterpieces. He was thirty-five.

A colleague and rival composer in Vienna, Antonio Salieri, who was generally less talented than Mozart but more successful, confessed in later years to having poisoned Mozart. The fact that Mozart had remarked that he suspected he was being poisoned supports the claim. The controversy as to the actual cause of Mozart's death has raged for years and has been stirred up again recently by the play and movie versions of Peter Schaffer's *Amadeus.*

Franz Peter Schubert 1797-1828

Schubert lived for only thirty-one years. As in the case of Mozart, we cannot help but wonder what glories of music Schubert would have left had he lived longer. We can be thankful, however, that in the short time he had, he worked constantly and left a rich sample of the unique and alluring fruits of his genius.

Though many great composers eventually came to live in Vienna, Schubert was actually born in the city where his father was a teacher in a boy's school. Like Haydn before him, Schubert served as a choirboy until his voice changed. A scholarship allowed him to stay on playing violin in the orchestra. He then began work as a teacher in his father's school, but was poorly suited for the post and quit at the age of twenty-one. This was no doubt partly because he was infatuated with writing music; he had already completed more than 300 compositions before he was twenty. Many of these were songs, a form for which he had an incomparable gift and is credited with perfecting. Other composers, Beethoven and Mozart among them, had occasionally written songs, but Schubert's songs illuminated the poetry; they were unforgettable small mas-

terpieces.   Some, like his *Serenade* and *Ave Maria* are
among the best known works in all of music.

Aside from the love and admiration of a close circle of
friends he never attained even a modest financial success.
He lived a bohemian life, staying for a while with one
friend and then with another, selling his priceless songs to
publishers for pitifully small amounts.   Though he never
earned enough to buy or even rent a piano, he did earn a
reputation as a songwriter.   Even Beethoven, whom
Schubert came to idolize, was impressed with his work.
But Schubert was much too shy to make contact; he visited
the great composer only once, just before Beethoven's
death.

In addition to songs, he wrote music in all current
forms of the age, though many of the large works were

never performed during his lifetime, including his last and greatest symphonies, the "*Unfinished*" and the "*Great*" C Major.

Beethoven died in 1827 and Schubert followed one year later, succumbing to typhoid fever. Near death, his friends said, he lamented that new ideas - ideas that would never be written - were constantly running through his head.

Robert Schumann 1810-1856

Schumann was the embodiment of the Romantic spirit, in his life and in his work. Because he is the most personal of composers, his music directly reflects everything he thought and felt. To listen with an open heart to his finest music can be an absorbing experience.

His father was a bookseller in Zwickau, Germany, and from him Robert developed a love of literature and poetry. A talented young pianist, he began law school only to drop out, convincing his mother that he could make a career in music. He studied with Friedrich Wieck, a musician and teacher of piano. Wieck's 9-year old daughter, Clara, was already a gifted virtuoso pianist when she first met the eighteen-year-old Schumann. One of the problems of piano technique is establishing independence of the fingers. To acheive this, Schumann, with characteristic over-enthusiasm, invented a device that immobilized his fingers by turns while he practiced. Unfortunately this device caused permanent damage to one of his fingers, ending all hopes of a concert career.

Schumann now turned his attention to composing and to several other projects. He began a twice-weekly publication, the *New Journal for Music,* for which he did most of the writing.   It was in this publication that he would introduce the young Johannes Brahms to the musical world.   Schumann was both intelligent and literate and the "Journal" exerted a strong influence on musical thought of the time.

In the meantime, he and Clara, despite their nine year difference in age, had fallen in love. They became engaged when Clara was seventeen, but her father strongly opposed the match, and they were forced to go to court for permission to marry.   They did, in fact, have a highly successful marriage and raised six children. The Schumann house was a center for intellectual and artistic discussion and activity. Brahms, who had been helped in his career by Schumann's support, became a close friend of the family and lived with them for a time.

Schumann had always been highly sensitive and moody, but in 1851 he began to suffer hallucinations.   In 1854 he attempted to drown himself and, soon thereafter, voluntarily entered an asylum where he died two years later at the age of 46.

Igor Stravinsky 1882-1971

Stravinsky's creative career spanned the better part of the twentieth century.   Throughout that time he was generally regarded as the world's leading composer.   Not content to rest on his successes, however, just when the musical world would come around to first accepting and then acclaiming his last seemingly outrageous shift in style, he would shift in another direction, continually unsettling the musical world throughout his long and distinguished career.

Stravinsky's father was the leading basso of the opera at St. Petersburg in Russia, but as is the case with a great many composers, he encouraged his son to study law.   And as is also often the case, Igor neglected his legal studies and spent his time on music.   At twenty-one, Stravinsky became a student of Nikolai Rimsky-Korsakov, the famous Russian composer of the Romantic style.

Serge Diaghilev was the director of the famous *Russian Ballet* which was based in Paris.   On a trip to Russia he heard a composition by the young Stravinsky and engaged him to provide new music for his dancers.   His first major work, a ballet called *The Firebird*, was in a new, un-refined and primitive sounding style, but it was nevertheless greeted with great success and his career was launched.

In 1913, however, the story was different: the premier of his new ballet, *The Rite of Spring*, was too brutal-sounding and unconventional even for the sophisticated Parisian audience. A real riot erupted and Stravinsky had to sneak out through a basement window in fear of being beaten. It took a number of years, but it was not too long before the world recognized that the "Rite" was in fact a great work, a classic, and Stravinsky's fame was reaffirmed.

He lived in Switzerland during World War I, with his wife and children. After the Russian Revolution of 1917 he became an exile in France. His music now changed to a cooler, more restrained style, strongly influenced by classical and sometimes Baroque music. Audiences were late in appreciating his innovations, preferring the "old" Stravinsky to the new, but catching up eventually.

With World War II, he moved to the United States, settling in California. He had always strongly opposed the 12 tone method of composition developed by Arnold Schoenberg, but in the 1950s - again to the great shock and dismay of his followers - he adopted the method. As long as he believed in it, his powerful individuality, lively intelligence and astounding musical skills could serve to make any style the basis for great music.

He died in 1971 at the age of eighty-eight, the most famous and most successful composer of the century.

Peter Iliyich Tchaikowsky 1840-1893

Painfully shy, somewhat neurotic and overly sensitive, from a private life tinged with social and emotional distress, Tchaikowsky succeeded in evoking some of the world's most popular and best loved music. Composing in a supersensuous and quintessentially Late Romantic style, he is recognized as the greatest of the Russian composers.

Tchaikowsky was trained in law and held a position as a clerk in the Ministry of Justice when, at the age of twenty-one, he decided to study music at the conservatory in St. Petersburg. Always a quick learner, he progressed so rapidly that the following year he left his job to study full time and upon graduating took a position as Professor of Harmony at the Moscow Conservatory. He worked at composition and by the age of thirty had produced the overture-fantasy *Romeo and Juliet*, his first great creation.

1877 was eventful for Tchaikowsky. The thirty seven year old professor agreed to marry a young student from the conservatory who was infatuated with him and his music. Tchaikowsky was homosexual, a secret source of great anguish to him in that highly repressive Victorian age, and he probably hoped that he could somehow make things work out in the marriage and at least present a respectable appearance. The marriage was a disaster and Tchaikowsky attempted to end his life by wading into a river to catch pneumonia. He survived, however, though separated from his wife, who, as it turned out, had considerable emotional problems of her own.

That same year Tchaikowsky began to receive an annuity from a rich widow who admired him and loved his music. Her name was Nadejda von Meck and she stipulated that she and Tchaikowsky would communicate by letter, but never meet. Her annuity freed the composer to resign his teaching position and to concentrate on creating. A peculiar, intimate relationship was established between them lasting for fourteen years, during which Tchaikowsky turned out a steady stream of masterful and mature works.

In 1893, internationally famous and respected, he accepted an invitation to conduct his work at the opening of Carnegie Hall in New York. Later that same year he finished his last symphony, the *"Pathetique,"* with its mournful, despairing last movement. It was, as Tchaikowsky described it, a program symphony but with a program that would remain secret. Its tragic and sorrowful atmosphere and the fact that hidden in the texture of the symphony are phrases of the Russian Requiem Mass, indicate that the composer was thinking of ending his life. Less than a week after the premiere, he was dead. Officially, the cause was ascribed to drinking unboiled water during a cholera epidemic, but some evidence indicates that the composer poisoned himself to avoid the threat of a homosexual relationship being publicly exposed.

Giuseppe Verdi 1813-1901

Aside from his great *Requiem Mass*, everything of significance that Verdi wrote was for the opera house. He is the prototype of the Italian Opera composer and deservedly so. Mozart is his only rival in the phenomenal ability to distill human feelings into exquisite, expressive musical phrases. He said that he wrote for the masses, and the masses love his music; but somehow beneath the surface of what appear to be simple, almost naive tunes, is a hidden depth, an uncanny capacity to reflect the true and profound currents of the human condition that we all share.

He was the son of an illiterate tavern keeper in a small Italian village. His talent for music was discovered early and at the age of 10 he was sent off to study in a nearby city. By the time he was twenty-two, he had finished his studies in Milan with the support of a wealthy patron.

He returned to the town of Busetto. He had been in love with the daughter of his patron and a position as music director allowed them to marry. Within a few years he moved his family back to Milan, where he had a success with his first opera, produced at La Scala. His career seemed assured when illness took the lives of his two young children and his wife. He was, deeply depressed and when his next opera failed, he gave up composing.

An inspiring libretto put him back to work and the opera *Nabucco* resulted. The subject was the enslavement of the Jews by the wicked Nebuchadnezzar. Since Italy was suffering under the rule of Austria at the time, the opera became a symbol of Italy's struggle for self-determination and Verdi found himself a national hero, a role in keeping with his beliefs and a responsibility that he bore with great honor. The cry was frequently heard, "*Viva Verdi*," which also secretly stood for the outlawed patriotic sentiment, "*Vittorio Emmanuele Re D'Italia*" (Victor Emmanuel, King of Italy).

A series followed, when he was in his late thirties, of three immortal masterworks; *Rigoletto*, *Il Trovatore* and *La Traviata*. In the end, wealthy and famous, he remarried and continued a fruitful life, composing his last great opera, *Falstaff*, at the age of seventy-nine.

Richard Wagner 1813-1883

Wagner is well known to have been mean, selfish, opportunistic, profligate, licentious, greedy, avaricious, self indulgent and arrogant. This is rare among great composers, who may have had failings and weaknesses but were, on the whole, essentially good human beings. We would like to be able to dismiss Wagner as unworthy, but he was also a blazing genius, one of the most influential individuals in history, and a composer of great operas.

Born in Leipzig, Germany, he was one of the few composers who did not learn to perform on any instrument. What he did learn about music, aside from a short course in harmony, he taught himself.   His university years were spent on carousing, drinking, gambling, acquiring debts that he would never repay and taking advantage of practically everyone he met.

He married an actress and began conducting in small towns.   A move to Paris in 1839 landed him in debtor's prison, but then his opera, *Rienzi* was successfully produced in Dresden and he was appointed conductor in that city.   Even though he had a good income he continued to live beyond his means, amassing tremendous debt, and was finally forced to flee to Switzerland to avoid arrest.

He now spent three years writing, not music, but prose; books about philosophy and art, particularly about the art of opera which he preferred to call "music drama," stressing the importance of the dramatic elements. He also completed writing the libretto for a cycle of four operas to be known as *The Ring of the Nibelung*, based on Norse mythology.

Wagner's fortunes improved in 1864 when the eighteen year old "mad king" Ludwig of Bavaria, who was an ardent admirer of Wagner, offered almost unlimited financial support to produce his operas. The composition and production of several more operas followed, including the completion of the music for "The Ring" operas.

In his private life, Wagner had fallen in love with Cosima von Bulow, the daughter of the great composer-pianist Franz Liszt and the wife of Wagner's close friend, the conductor Hans von Bulow. She had two children by Wagner while still married to von Bulow and then married Wagner when his first wife died.

"The Ring" was premiered in 1876 in a theater specially designed by Wagner and constructed in the Bavarian town of Bayreuth. His operas are still presented there today.

Reflecting his philosophy of what he called the "music of the future," Wagner's operas are characterized by an extended musical line that does away with the conventional division into arias and recitatives; there is much of what he called "speech-song," which follows the natural cadence of language; and the orchestra plays a more important role in contributing to the drama.   Characters and ideas can be called to mind by the appearance in the orchestra of special, short musical mottos or *leitmotifs*, which are associated with them.

Wagner's last opera, Parsifal was completed in 1882. Having convinced the world of his greatness, he died of a heart attack at the age of 69 and was buried near his festival theater in Bayreuth.

CHAPTER ELEVEN

Recordings And Stereo Equipment

It may seem obvious that an important element in listening to music is being able to hear it clearly, with full dynamic range, accurate colors, and no distortion. Art music can make the greatest demands on stereo equipment with frequent contrast in range, dynamics, and texture. In fact, it is not unusual to find enthusiastic listeners whose introduction to art music came by way of an interest in stereo equipment. Testing the limits of a fine stereo system inevitably leads to recordings of some of the great works of tremendous sonic power containing extremes of high and low, with great and sometimes sudden contrast between the softest, most delicate sounds and thundering volumes: *Requiems* by Berlioz and Verdi, or Tchaikowsky's *1812 Overture*, for example.

A problem already mentioned is that many listeners are accustomed to poor recording quality and have a wrong impression of the way art music can and should sound. Because of the sonic demands of most art music there can be a great deal of distortion if the recording or playback system is not adequate. After years of hearing art music played on notoriously limited TV sets, especially never having experienced a live performance, it is understandable that some listeners have the idea and expectation that orchestral music is, by nature, thin sounding, muddy and distorted.

Fortunately we live in a time when it does not require a large investment to enjoy an extremely high level of sound reproduction. The last ten years - first with digital recordings, and then compact disks - have brought tremendous advances in making high quality sound very affordable.

As a guide for acquiring a quality stereo setup at a reasonable price, this chapter will provide a quick run-through of basic concepts of stereo equipment.

A Quick History of Sound Recording and Reproduction

All sound is vibration. When Thomas Edison first conceived the phonograph, it was a basic way of transferring those vibrations to a physical medium for storage and then back again, later, into vibrations.

Edison's machine consisted of a brass cylinder covered with a thin sheet of tin foil. Touching the tin foil was a needle attached to a diaphragm at the end of a funnel. Turning the handle caused the cylinder to rotate, and, because it was mounted on a threaded rod, it slowly traveled from side to side, with the needle tracing a spiral path around the cylinder.

Edison describes what happened:

> "...I designed a little machine using a cylinder provided with grooves around the surface. Over this was to be placed tinfoil, which easily received and recorded the movements of the diaphragm. A sketch was made. The workman who got the sketch was John Kreusi. I didn't have much faith that [the "talking machine"] would work, expecting that I might possibly hear a word or so that would give hope of a future for the idea. Kreusi, when he had nearly finished it, asked what it was for. I told him I was

going to record talking, and then have the machine talk back. He thought it absurd. However it was finished, the foil was put on; I then shouted 'Mary had a little lamb,' etc. I adjusted the reproducer, and the machine reproduced it perfectly. I was never so taken aback in my life. Everybody was astonished."

Edison's original sketch for the "Talking Machine."

The term given to this kind of recording is **"analog,"** because the vibrations are encoded in patterns, physical hills and valleys, in this case, that are "analogous" to, that is, they resemble, the shapes of the vibrations of the source sounds. The pattern of vibrations in its recorded or encoded form is referred to as the **"signal."**

Edison's invention was revolutionary, but the sound quality was limited. Recording of the vibrations was only approximate because the recording equipment did not vibrate precisely like the source, due to the inefficiency of the process. There was a loss of **fidelity** or accuracy in the reproduction. This also caused the recording to be limited in volume. The laws of nature dictate that the playback must always be less loud than the original due to inevitable loss of energy in the process, and in this rudimentary arrangement that loss was considerable, but improvements followed.

First came the switch from turning the cylinder by hand, to a spring mechanism. The machine was wound with a crank and then the mechanism rotated the cylinder at a constant rate of speed. RCA Victor then introduced a competing system that used flat discs in place of cylinders. These were what we have come to know as records. The first ones rotated at a speed of 78 rotations per minute (RPMs).

The next major innovation was the addition of an electrical component called an **"amplifier"** that would amplify the vibrations as they came from the needle (or stylus, as it is alternately known) and convert them into pulses of electrical current which would then be fed to an electrically operated loudspeaker. The listener could now control the loudness of the playback.

In the early 1950s LPs, or long playing records, were introduced. These rotated at a speed of 33 $1/3$ RPM and allowed up to 30 minutes on one side of a record as opposed to just five minutes on the 78s. This was the era of "high fidelity," and many small improvements in all aspects of recording combined to greatly improve sound quality.

Another major innovation that appeared in the '50s was stereophonic sound. This involved recording a performance using two microphones, encoding the vibrational patterns on two tracks, both carried together in the groove of the record, and then playing back through two amplifiers and two speakers. The most obvious result of stereo sound was that it gave the effect of spreading the sound of the performing group laterally across the playback area. Many recordings of ping-pong games and trains coming in from the left and speeding off to the right were sold in the 1950s so that people could enjoy their new stereos. Since there is not a great deal of moving around on the stage during the performance of most music, the effect of stereo might be thought to be of small significance.

What many fail to realize, however, because it is a much less obvious effect, is that in addition to the lateral spreading of the sound there is also a more subtle, but very important expansion of the feeling of depth. It is similar to the stereoscopic or 3D visual effect. We have only two eyes and only two ears, but both of these biological systems are designed to supply the brain with information about a third dimension: depth. For listening to music this can add a discreet, but very enriching feeling of the acoustical environment. We are no longer listening to music emanating from a flat plane. Now we experience the ambience, the openness, of the hall in which the performance took place. One musician described it as, "that nice airy stereo sound." (It can be hard to hear this effect. If you listen to music on equipment that has a feature that allows switching back and forth from stereo to mono [monaural sound], and you do this while listening on headphones, the difference will be more discernable and apparent.)

Recording and playback on tape became available first on what were called, reel-to-reel tape recorders, and then in the more convenient cassette format. Both of these systems work by translating the vibrational patterns, not into physical hills and valleys, but into magnetic patterns along a length of tape.

The seventies brought the advent of digital recording and computer technology, making it possible to translate vibrational patterns into numerical (digital) codes. These digital codes are more accurate than the previous analog system and have the advantage of being transferable from one medium to another with absolutely no deterioration. In addition, the digital process does not involve the inevitable underlying noise level always found in analog recordings. Along with, or as a result of the digital process came a new medium to go with the new method: the compact disc, or CD.

With the CD came a great number of advantages: more total time than a record - over an hour on one side as opposed to less than an hour divided between the two sides of a record; CDs provide immediate access to the material anywhere in the recording, which is a significant advantage over cassettes; no noise level; and because the code is buried beneath the surface of the disc, sandwiched between substantial layers of plastic, they are impervious to dust and minor scratches. All indications are that CDs will prove to be much more permanent and less vulnerable to damage than the older media.

Of course the big advantage is the quality of sound. When you start a CD there is no clunk, no hiss, no buzz or hum - nothing - that is until the music begins, which it does out of complete silence; and then we hear clear sound with no distortion and a larger range of dynamics - the softs are softer and the louds are louder. Many listeners notice that listening is more comfortable, free of the fatigue that used to come with the almost imperceptible but ever-present hiss or noise level. Due to the greater dynamic range, it is also possible to listen at a lower overall dynamic level and still feel the force and power of the louder sections.

In short the CD has brought us to a golden age of sound. It is, however, still possible to run into problems if the rest of the system is not capable of quality reproduction. No matter how wonderful a CD is, a stereo system is only as strong as its weakest link.

What to Look For in a Stereo System

Of course the surest way to get a good system is to spend a lot of money. If you have several thousand dollars for equipment you will almost certainly end up with fine sound. But if your budget is more limited there are things that you need to consider.

It is very attractive, when shopping for a sound system, to focus on an all-in-one system. These are units that sell for up to several hundred dollars and usually include a turntable on top, AM-FM radio, cassette player, possibly a CD player, and two detachable speakers. Included, of course, is some sort of amplifier. The trouble with these sets is that they are usually not capable of quality sound because the amplifier and speakers are insufficient. Feel the weight of the speakers. If they are light or flimsy they will produce distortion. Ask about the power rating of the amplifier. If it is not indicated, that is a sure sign that it is inadequate.

A better idea is to invest in a component system. This involves finding separate units that fit your budget and needs. The arrangement can be updated and improved by adding or replacing the individual parts, if and when you can afford it and as the need arises.

The foundation of the system is the amplifier and speakers.   Without quality here, good sound will be impossible.   Once these are in place it will be possible to plug in tapes, records, or CDs, even from portable players, and still have very good sound.

Speakers
Generally, larger speakers have more capacity than small ones, especially in reproducing the deep bass tones. There are, however, many excellent speakers available in small sizes and at reasonable prices: under one hundred dollars each.   Speakers need to withstand substantial vibration without adding vibrations of their own, so they must be made of strong and rigid material.   Good speakers feel hefty and solid when they are picked up.

If you happen to be short of funds, you can get the rest of your system and put off buying speakers for awhile, choosing, temporarily, to listen on good quality headphones that deliver excellent sound at far less cost.

Amplifiers or Receivers
Amplifiers are rated in watts per channel, with two channels required for stereo.   Fifteen watts per channel will provide adequate sound.   Very powerful amplifiers, one hundred watts per channel or higher, deliver clear, clean sound even in highly complex passages and at the loudest volumes, but it may not be worth the higher cost.   You will probably do well to start with an amplifier with a rating of twenty-five to thirty-five watts per channel.   This will provide a very good, satisfying quality of sound in a fairly large room at minimum cost.

Our approach is aimed at gathering a system of individual components, but it makes sense to compromise this approach to accommodate an idiosyncrasy of the stereo trade: A **tuner** is a component that receives radio broadcasts.   A **receiver** is a component that combines a tuner with an amplifier.   Because more receivers are made and sold than amplifiers or tuners, prices are lower and you can pay less for this combination component than either a tuner or an amplifier bought separately and still have excellent quality.

In summary then, it is recommended that you look for a receiver with a power rating of twenty-five to thirty-five watts per channel.   Together with speakers or headphones this establishes the basis of the system.   So far though, the only thing that can be heard will be radio broadcasts. Missing are additional components to decode signals from recordings.   LP records and the turntables required to play them are rapidly becoming things of the past.   What is needed is a CD player.

CD Players
CDs use a laser beam to read the signal.   If a CD player works at all it will sound very good; it is inherent in the design.   It is not necessary to look for elaborate features. Unless you insist on having remote control or automatic changing devices, things that have no effect on the actual sound, an excellent quality CD player can be found for about one hundred dollars.

Tape Players
A cassette player is a useful addition to the basic system, both to play cassettes and to make recordings, either from the radio or from CDs.   Recording directly

from a CD, by the way, produces an amazingly good quality recording. This is being written at a period of transition in tape equipment. A new product known as DAT, standing for digital audio tape is just becoming available. This exciting development combines the advantages of cassettes and CDs. Like cassettes, it is possible to record on DAT, either with a microphone, or direct from another recording through the system's amplifier. Like CDs, DAT uses digital, not analog, technology, and produces excellent recordings with no deterioration of the signal and no tape hiss or noise level. DAT uses mini cassettes, smaller and more convenient than normal cassettes, and thanks to a new transport system with a revolving spiral tape head, there is more material on less tape and improved ability to access the tape quicker, without waiting for rewinding.

DAT is new, and at this writing, available but expensive. New technology tends to lower in price rapidly and there is no doubt that within a short time DAT players will be much more affordable. In short, it could be a mistake to invest in a conventional cassette player at this time. A system with a CD player and a DAT cassette player is probably all anyone will really need for the foreseeable future and the quality of sound from a system like this would have been undreamed of a decade ago.

An entirely adequate component system can be had for about one hundred dollars per unit, that is: two speakers, a receiver, a CD player and, no doubt in a short time, a DAT player, five units - five hundred dollars. Take off 20 to 40 percent if you are good at finding sales or if you can drive a hard bargain.

On Choosing Recordings

Browsing in a record store (we still call them record stores even though they rarely sell records anymore) for something that looks interesting is one of the great pleasures, and can be wonderful for developing a sense of the scope of music literature. If, however, you are looking for a recording of a particular work you should consult the Schwann Catalog. Something like a "Books in Print" for recordings, this monthly publication lists every tape or CD currently available with all pertinent information. You should be able to buy one at the record store or just consult the store's copy.

In choosing a performance there are some things to look for. As might be expected, the more expensive recordings are usually better. The bargain priced recordings tend to be either less than top notch performances or re-releases of older recordings. Sometimes there are good reasons for preferring an older recording. It may be a historic performance by a legendary artist. Recordings by the great conductor Arturo Toscanini are a case in point. The inspiration and excitement in these performances is extraordinary, and often make up for limited fidelity. In general, however, you should probably look for a newer recording.

CDs usually include a three letter code on the package to provide information about the recording, "A" standing for analog, "D" standing for Digital; AAD, ADD or DDD. The code gives details about the phases of the recording process in this order: original recording/mastering/format. The newest, cleanest sound is provided through the completely digital configuration, or DDD. AAD indicates a recording from before the digital era.

CHAPTER TWELVE

Concertgoing

The real reason to go to a concert is to listen to the music. Even with today's spectacular digital recordings, the ultimate musical experience is still a live performance. There is the unpredictability and excitement of having the music created right there, an intangible sense that this is the forum for which the music was conceived, the natural habitat.

There are peripheral things as well. For centuries art music was at home in the royal courts of Europe. The spirit of elegance and nobility is inherent in much of the music itself, but it is also to be found in the cultured aura and physical surroundings of the concert hall, in the ambiance, the architecture, the furnishings and exhibits. All told, these elements contribute to an experience that, in totality, can be wonderfully different, welcome and refreshing. It is also reassuring, in our frenetic and in many ways neurotic society, that there are still many -

hundreds and thousands - who find it worthwhile to take part in this ancient ritual of gathering in a large place to sit quietly while the patterns of vibrations that we call music take their mysterious and wonderful effect.

Where to Find Information on Concerts

To find information about what concerts will be presented in your area first look in the Sunday Arts and Leisure section of the local newspaper. You will find listings of concerts that are coming up immediately and also details on concerts that are scheduled for the future. If you do not find complete information, call or visit the box office of a major music hall, arts center or theater where concerts are given. They will probably be able to provide details on all scheduled performances.

There are a number of reasons that it is important to arrange to go to a live performance well ahead of time. The best reason reflects ideas in Chapter One; the importance of preparing and becoming familiar with the program. Tickets can be expensive, as we will discuss soon, and attending unprepared will certainly not yield maximum value. Waiting too long to arrange for tickets can also mean finding the performance sold out. Unlike movies that repeat for weeks and months, a concert is often presented only once, and if it happens to be sold out there may not be another alternative. Particularly attractive concerts involving great performers, especially popular pieces or special events, frequently sell out the day that tickets go on sale, just as in rock music. And just as in rock music there are sometimes scalpers willing to sell tickets at above official prices.

A friend who lives near Lincoln Center maintains that he has shown up at the last minute on hundreds of evenings and has never failed to get in to something for a reasonable price. He maintains that though there are scalpers, there are also people who arrive with extra tickets because someone could not attend . These people are usually glad to let these tickets go for less than the official price. If you should see someone walking slowly near the ticket window holding tickets conspicuously fanned out in a slightly unnatural position, looking directly at you with eyebrows raised and ever so slightly shaking this head meaningfully up and down; and if you should ask this person if he or she might possibly happen to have an extra ticket or two, you should not be surprised to find that he or she does, indeed, etc.

On Choosing Concerts

Most communities offer a wide array of concerts to choose from. Among them are local amateur, semi-professional, church, school, and university performances. These performers are a great local resource and often present highly commendable performances. They are sometimes free or very reasonably priced. College students in particular are often urged to attend the performances given by the college music department. There may be good reasons of a social or academic nature to do this. ALL OF THE ABOVE NOTWITHSTANDING, if you are serious about really learning to love music, DO NOT CHOOSE THESE CONCERTS. There is a tremendous gap between amateur and professional performance. Especially in the beginning stages, when you are forming important opinions about music and your own reaction to it, you should insist on attending the highest level professional performance available. There are very few places in the Western World that are not within driving distance of a major city with a nationally recognized orchestra; many of these orchestras tour extensively. The cost of these concerts will naturally be higher, but well worth the price.

Choosing Seats

Ticket prices are usually established with care and you get what you pay for. The best and most expensive seats are probably not in the front row. The box office has a seating chart, usually well worked out, with the most expensive seats having the best view and the best acoustics; not too close and not too far away. On the one hand you might say that a seat is a seat and get the most reasonable available. On the other hand, keep in mind that many concert halls and opera houses are very large. If you are stuck up in the rafters you may be too far from the performers to see well, or more important, to hear well. Veteran concert-goers bring binoculars or opera glasses which can be very helpful especially with opera and ballet, where the visual dimension is very important, particularly if your seat is far from the stage.

If you have prepared well for the concert, you have already made a big investment in the evening. As a result you can expect considerable return in the form of a powerful, engaging and highly rewarding experience. In this case it probably makes sense to invest a little more and pay for as good a seat as you can reasonably afford. If this still leaves you in the cheap seats you will at least be in good company. As a rule the most dedicated, avid and honestly enthusiastic listeners are found in these sections. Sometimes, depending upon the rules of the hall and the diligence of the ushers, it is possible, once everyone is seated, to notice where there are good empty seats and to inconspicuously relocate.

If you plan to dine out before the concert, choosing a restaurant near the concert hall is a good idea as these places are usually accustomed to getting people out in time for the performance.

Take care to arrive on time. The days are over when society ladies could arrive late so that everyone would notice their entrance. Today if you arrive late, the ushers will not seat you while the performance is under way. You will have to wait until there is a substantial break, between scenes or movements; in some programs this can be quite a long time.

What to Wear to the Concert

There was a time when it was expected that concert audiences would be formally dressed. This is no longer true.   You will still find concertgoers in gowns and tuxedoes, and if you enjoy a chance to get dressed up, this would be a good opportunity.   But you will also see many in business dress or even reasonably casual clothing.   In general, people feel that being at least moderately well-dressed is most comfortable and appropriate.

In the early sixties the author, as a high school student, was chosen to represent his school in a program that included attending a series of concerts presented at the Juilliard School of Music.   The composer William Schuman was then the president of the Juilliard School and there was a rule that men were required to wear ties at concerts.   At one of the evening performances those gentlemen without ties were asked to leave their seats and were allowed to listen to the concert standing in the rear of the hall.   Two individuals were discovered without the proper neckwear; the author and a very seedy looking old man with a flannel shirt and much wild, Einstein-like white hair.   We two listened from the back, consoling one another in exile.   The first work on the program was an exciting piece by the modern composer and pioneer of electronic music, Edgard Varese.   When the piece ended, as often happens, the conductor had been made aware that the composer was expected to be in the audience and during the applause he peered out into the hall motioning for the composer to stand and be recognized.   The composer was not in his seat but was eventually located standing in the rear together with a high school student.

As you are seated you will probably be given a program containing information on the performers, the pieces and the order in which they will be presented.   Since you will probably have been thoroughly prepared and familiar with the compositions it will not be crucial to read this but there may be some interesting new things. Do not wait to read the program until the performance is in progress, however, because the lights will be turned off when the music starts.

It is customary not to applaud between movements of a work. The number of movements can be determined from the program. If you are an inexperienced concertgoer the best policy is not to be the first to applaud. In opera, however, audiences do applaud (and yell and carry on) after well sung arias or ensembles.

Those who do not frequently attend art music performances are usually surprised at the intensity of the audiences silence. This is for two reasons: first, the performers are involved in highly demanding efforts requiring the greatest concentration. Secondly, many in the audience are listening with great intensity. They love the music deeply and are not happy with noise or distractions.

CHAPTER THIRTEEN
Historically Authentic Performances

Until very recently the music of past ages was performed in many respects very much like more recent music. Musicians, especially the better, more sensitive performers, did recognize that there were appropriate styles for performing the music of different ages. They would approach Mozart, for instance, with a more refined, neater touch than they would approach a Late Romantic composer like Rachmaninoff, whose music demanded more power, flexibility and romantic abandon. Some of this was done naturally, by intuition, and some was studied and taught: how trills were performed differently in the Baroque and Romantic periods, for instance.

But attention to the fine details of authentic performance practice was limited. The keyboard music of Bach, for instance, has been routinely performed on the modern piano, even though the piano was just being invented during Bach's lifetime and his music was written for the harpsichord. Likewise, Bach's orchestra music has been played by full scale, modern symphony orchestras even though Bach's own orchestras were one third as large and the construction of the instruments of his time produced substantially different sounds and textures.

Somehow the feeling was that instruments and performance in general had improved steadily over time and if Bach or Handel could have heard their music played by our modern piano or orchestra, of course they would have loved it.

Gradually the weight of opinion began to shift away from this attitude as this century progressed, and by the 1970s, pockets of musicians had sprung up in many cities who were dedicated to, and specialized in, performing early music on authentic, period instruments in historically accurate style.

At first these were considered oddities and only attracted the interest of musicologists and listeners thought to have unusual musical tastes. This was easy to believe since, in the beginning, when performers were rediscovering the techniques of building and playing the old instruments, they made some really crude, rough sounding and out of tune music.

As they persisted in using the old techniques, however, the sounds became more controlled and the musical world was forced to listen and admit that there was something to this approach.

To cite one example: There had always been much discussion on the proper use of ornaments in Baroque music in general, but especially in Baroque keyboard music. It was a complex subject because Baroque composers expected performers to add ornaments improvisationally, and did not notate them. There were, however, Baroque treatises that went into great detail about when to ornament and how; but always calling for discretion and taste on the part of the performer. This left room for debates and disagreements about what was too much ornamentation and what was too little, etc.

When Baroque keyboard music began to be performed as it was intended, on the harpsichord rather than on the piano, it threw great light on the subject of ornaments. The tone of a note struck on the piano lasts much longer than a note struck on the harpsichord. We say that the harpsichord has a quick "decay factor." A composer might conceive of a musical phrase containing a long note such as could be sung or played on an instrument capable of sustaining a long tone, like the violin. If this phrase were played on the harpsichord, however, the long note would quickly decay and appear to be followed by an emptiness. In order to avoid this, the harpsichordist would invent or improvise ornaments to fill the gap and extend the melodic impetus to the next note in the phrase. When performed on the harpsichord, the need for ornaments became clear and suddenly made sense.

Other aspects of Baroque performance were illuminated by the use of authentic instruments. The timbre of the period instruments was considerably lighter, somewhat thinner and more transparent. This, together with the authentic practice of using smaller numbers of instruments, resulted in performances of wonderful clarity. Complex

Baroque polyphony which had sounded heavy, obscure and muddy, became light and clear; suddenly you could hear all the parts.

An esoteric question concerns pitch level. Our modern notes sound higher than the same note in the Baroque Period did. Modern "A" vibrates at an international standard of 440 cycles per second. Baroque "A" varied considerably from time to time and place to place, but the average was 415 cycles per second. This is actually very close to our modern "A flat," or one note (technically a half step) lower. Some musicians maintain that pitch levels are relative and that modern pitch ought to be used for all music, but most Baroque specialists maintain that there are subtle but important distinctions and that the instruments and voices sound fuller and more comfortable at the lower, authentic pitch.

So there is still a debate about the quest for authenticity in performance practice, some arguing that it is an impossible goal because research can never tell with real certainty how Baroque music actually sounded. It is said that ultimately the performer must make subjective decisions based on what sounds best. What sounds best, however, is most often in keeping with what research tells us, and the period instrument players have, by now, found a real place in modern musical life. Listeners are often not sure they like the new, authentic sound at first, but after hearing it, few can return to the sound of Baroque music on modern instruments. One result is that the standard, modern-instrument symphony orchestras that are so prominently a part of musical life have essentially stopped playing Baroque music; this is now left to the specialized period instrument ensembles.

Following is a description of some instruments that will be encountered in authentic, period performances and how they differ from modern instruments.

Baroque Violin

The great violin makers - Amati, Stradivarius, and Guarnerius - actually lived in the early Baroque Period; it is the instruments they made that have been the most treasured over the centuries and which are still being played today. So the modern violin was perfected in the Baroque Period. However, there have been some changes. For one thing, the strings were made of gut; newer strings are metal wound and can stand higher tension. As a result modern instruments have a slightly longer neck that is set more at an angle. Baroque specialists use gut strings and the original shorter, straighter neck. The Baroque bow, too, had a different design and produced a lighter sound.

Viola Da Gamba

The viols were a family of string instruments that, like the recorder, became extinct after the Baroque Period, being replaced by the fuller-sounding and more flexible violin family. The viols had sloping shoulders and used frets, like a guitar, to determine the placement of pitches on the fingerboard. The most common size, and a prominent instrument in period performances, was the viola da gamba, *gamba* meaning "leg" in Italian, because it was held supported by the legs like a 'cello, the instrument that eventually took its place.

Recorder & Flute

The most popular wind instrument in the Baroque era was the recorder, an instrument like the flute, but held vertically rather than horizontally. The tone is made by a whistle-like device called a "fipple." A rival instrument, the transverse flute, gained favor toward the late Baroque and developed into our modern flute. The recorder died out completely and was only revived in the mid-twentieth century. Although the modern flute is made of metal, in the Baroque era both the recorder and the flute were constructed of wood. The transverse flute had the advantage of a greater dynamic range and won out as performing groups grew larger toward the end of the Baroque Era.

Authentic Performance of Pre-Baroque Music

Some of the same problems attend music of the Renaissance and before, but not to the same degree. This music had always been the province of specialists and was different enough that, of necessity, it required special instruments and performance techniques. Since interest in this old music came so recently, there was not the conflict of an established practice of performance with modern instruments as there had been with Baroque music. There were and continue to be ensembles dedicated to performing the music of the Renaissance and before. They typically perform in period costume, often offer explanations of the proceedings, display an array of fascinating and exotic instruments and provide an altogether stimulating and entertaining time.

Period Performances of Classical and Romantic Music

Once the performance of Baroque music on period instruments gained acceptance, the concept extended to the Classical and then to the Romantic period. If you were interested in buying a recording of the complete set of Beethoven symphonies, for example, you would have a choice: a set by a conventional orchestra, lets say the Chicago Symphony, or a set by one of the new, authentic instrument orchestras. Of course the closer to the present, the less marked are the differences in both instruments and performance practice. These developments have not had the effect of rendering the conventional performance of the music of these periods invalid, as was essentially the case with the Baroque, but it has produced enlightening insights and some excellent performances. It will be very interesting to watch the progress of this trend to see what develops from here.

Suggested Basic Repertoire

With the exception of Puccini's *La Boheme*, these are works by composers whose biographical sketches appear in Chapter Ten.

J.S. Bach.	*Mass in B Minor*
	Brandenberg Concerto #2 in F Major (concerto grosso)
	Toccata & Fugue in G Minor (organ)
	Passacaglia & Fugue in C Minor (Organ)
	English Suite #2 in A Minor (harpsichord)
Bartok.	*Concerto for Orchestra*
Beethoven.	*Sonata No. 8 in C Minor "Pathetique"* (piano)
	Egmont Overture
	Symphony #3 "Eroica"
	Symphony #5 in C minor
	Symphony #9 "Choral"
	Piano Concerto #5 "Emperor"
	String Quartet #14 in C Minor
Brahms.	*Symphony #3 in F Major*
	A German Requiem
	Sextet in G Major op. 36
Chopin.	*Préludes, op. 28* (piano)

Debussy.	*Prelude a L'apres midi d'une Faune [Prelude to the Afternoon of a Faun]* (tone poem) *Claire de lune [Moonlight]* (piano)
Handel.	*Messiah* (oratorio) *Water Music* (orchestra)
Haydn.	*Symphony #104 in D major "London"* *Quartet in D Major op. 76, #3 (Emperor)*
Mozart.	*Symphony #40 in G Minor* *Don Giovanni* (Opera) *Piano Concerto #20 in D minor*
Puccini.	*La Boheme* (Opera)
Schubert.	*Symphony #9 in C Major, "The Great"* *"An die Musik" [To Music]* (song) *"Der Erlkönig" [The Erlking]* (song) *Quintet in C Major*
Schumann.	*Kinderscenen for piano [Scenes from Childhood]*
Stravinsky.	*Le Sacre du Printemps [Rite of Spring]* (Ballet)
Tchaikowsky.	*Symphony #5 in E minor, op. 64* *Romeo & Juliet* (Overture-Fantasy) *The Nutcracker* (Ballet) *Concerto for Violin in D Major*
Verdi.	*La Traviata* (Opera)
Wagner.	*Lohengrin* (Opera)

Italian Musical Terms

Since the system of notation for music was developed largely in Italy, most commonly used musical terms are in the Italian Language. We are not concerned in this book with learning to read music, but a familiarity with these terms can be very useful. Concert programs and information on recordings list the Italian tempo markings of compositions and their movements to help the listener to know what is happening and when.

Dynamics

Fortissimo	*ff*	Very loud
Forte	*f*	loud
Mezzo-forte	*mf*	Somewhat loud
Mezzo-piano	*mp*	Somewhat soft
Piano	*p*	Soft
Pianissimo	*pp*	Very soft
Crescendo	<	Become louder
Diminuendo	>	Become softer

Tempo

Presto	
Vivo	Very fast
Vivace	
Allegro	Fast
Moderato	Moderately fast
Andante	Moderately slow
Adagio	Slow

Grave
Largo   Very slow
Lento

Tempo continued

Accelerando   Become faster
Ritardando   Become Slower
Rubato   Flexible tempo

Articulation

Legato   Smooth and connected
Staccato   Short and detached
Tenuto   Sustained

INDEX

About the Author

Dr. Robert Danziger holds a Ph.D. in music from New York University. He has been serving as Chairman of the music department at the University of Bridgeport in Connecticut where his music appreciation courses are much in demand. A previous book, *The Musical Ascent of Herman Being - a How-To Novel*, has been adopted by more than two hundred colleges and universities across the United States.

About *The Musical Ascent of Herman Being*

by Robert Danziger

What the students said:

- A fantastic learning experience. I really enjoyed this book.
- An insightful book. This book kept me awake.
- A practical guide to music with a touch of comedy, drama, mystery and romance. The ending was great.
- Entices the reader into a deeper, more sophisticated involvement with music.
- Hysterically funny.
- Brings the reader a true understanding of classical music.
- Delightful, innovative: And it works.
- The story was something I could relate to.
- Easy to read and yet not simple minded.
- A thoughtful. creatively written aid to entering the world of art music.
- It made me laugh.
- A sneaky way to get a point across. I recommend this book to everyone.
- Not the average textbook. It kept my interest and I seem to retain more information.
- Colorful and truly fun to read.
- It is everything the cover says it is (a rare accomplishment).
- Quick reading and easy to understand.
- A witty book which restores faith to the depressed music listener.
- This reading made the class worth enrolling in.

Among the Colleges and Universities Using
The Musical Ascent of Herman Being

Alaska Pacific University
Allbright College
Ashland Community College
Bergen Cnty. Comm. College
Bethel College
Bluffton College
Boise State University
Bradford College
Bradley University
Cal State, Hayward
Cal State, Dominguez Hills
Cal State, Stanislaus
Cal State, Sacramento
Calvin College
Catawba College
Cayuga Cnty. Comm. College
Centre College of Kentucky
Coker College
College of Idaho
College of Saint Rose
College of Wooster
College of Wooster
Columbia Basin College
Cuayahoga Community College
DePaul University
DePauw University
Diablo Valley College
Dixie College
Earlham College
Elmhurst College
Essex Community College
Eureka College
Florida International University
Fort Lewis College
Frederick Community College
Furman College
George Fox College
Georgia Southern College
Georgia State University
Gettysburg College
Grossmont Cuyamoca College
Gustavus Adolphus College
Hartnell College
Hesston College
Hope College
Indiana University
Keystone Jr. College,
Lincoln Memorial University
Lock Haven College
Los Medanos College
Louisiana College
Lynchburg College
Marshall University
Martin Methodist College
McNees State University
Miami University
Midwestern State University
Mississippi State University

Modesto Jr. College
Montclair State College
National University
Nazareth College
New Mexico State University
North Central University
Northern Michigan University
Northwest Community College
Ohio Wesleyan University
Olympic College
Pacific Union College
Paris Jr. College
Pennsylvania State University
Peru State College
Porterville College
Potomax State College
Providence College
Quincy College
Randolph Macon College
Reed College
Rutgers University
San Diego Mesa College
Santa Barbara Comm. College
Santa Clara University
Shippensburg University
Sioux Falls College
Southern Utah State College
St. Gregory's College
St. Lawrence University
St. Mary's College, CA
St. Mary's College, IN
St. Mary's College, NE
St. Mary's College. TX
St. Mary's University, TX
St. Xavier College
Stephen F Austin State U.
Tusculum College
University of Arizona
University of Bridgeport
University of Delaware
University of Houston
University of Montana
University of North Carolina
University of San Diego
University of South Carolina
University of Virginia
University of Western Florida
University of Wisconsin
University of Wyoming
Valpariso University
Virginia Intermont College
Virginia Tech
Waldorf College
Wayne State College
West Virginia Wesleyan U.
Westfield State College
William Woods College
Yakima Valley Comm. College

The Musical Ascent of Herman Being - A How-To Novel, offers an ingenious new method to reveal the hidden depth and beauty of great music.

Engaging, fun and easy to read, it is the story of Herman's seduction by fortune, friendship, food, the opposite sex, and of course great music. Presented are fascinating insights into the essential nature of music, inspiration, and at the same time, a practical guide for dealing with music in the real world. Here, for the first time, is an approach that establishes a theory and an actual process for learning to love music.

Ultimately, Herman and the reader, are offered the "secret" of finding great music as a life enriching experience; a revelation of such power and elegance, it leaves the reader wondering how it could have gone undiscovered for so long.

5½x8½*108 pages*Quality Paperback
ISBN 0-9613427-5-9
Jordan Press*$8.95

Order Form

To: Jordan Press, 359 Central Avenue, New Haven, CT 06515

Please rush me _____ copies of The Musical Ascent of Herman Being - A How-To Novel @ $8.95 each, plus $2.00 for postage and handling. Payment enclosed.

Name _____

Address _____